程標覽知悉父然滬伴市諒悉常列今隔兩
月你来寧寄父子之情覽亦远矣常修
佳⋯學社學習應理尊重自己之既為經歷
譽今為舖中服務應幫忙舖中一切功夫
年在於高上地位學習應尊重自己名
今你兄錦添寧管住意司理權你當伊弟
者帮助之各事聽命之司理有尽職守之
可為居職對住意尽力對顧客要至誠
忠厚亥易公平對舖中合伴好酌量和
藉可親對你每必須孝敬以報劬勞養

TONG

TONG

The Story of Tong Louie, Vancouver's Quiet Titan

E.G. PERRAULT

HARBOUR PUBLISHING

Contents

FIRST PAGE: TONG LOUIE WITH HIS FATHER'S DELIVERY TRUCK CIRCA 1925.

PREVIOUS PAGE: TONG WAS AWARDED THE ORDER OF BRITISH COLUMBIA, BC'S HIGHEST CIVIC HONOUR, IN JUNE 1991.

OPPOSITE: H.Y. LOUIE WITH HIS SONS TONG AND TIM CIRCA 1917.

PREVIOUS PAGE: ONE OF TONG'S
FEW CONCESSIONS TO LUXURY WAS A
HANDSOMELY APPOINTED OFFICE.

THIS PAGE: AS A TEENAGER TONG
SPENT MUCH OF HIS SPARE TIME
WORKING IN THE FAMILY
WAREHOUSE, BUT ALWAYS HAD A
FEW MOMENTS TO ENTERTAIN
A BABY BROTHER.

OPPOSITE: A FORMER HIGH SCHOOL
ATHLETE, TONG STARTED JOGGING
FOR EXERCISE LONG BEFORE IT
BECAME FASHIONABLE. INTO HIS
SEVENTIES, HE REGULARLY JOGGED
THREE TO FIVE KILOMETRES IN
STANLEY PARK.

Introduction

A thoughtful observer might have learned much about Tong Louie's life by going to his funeral, which took place at St. Andrews Wesley Church in Vancouver on May 4, 1998. A bright sun lit up the snow-capped peaks of the North Shore mountains as a long line of mourners spilled down the church steps, out onto the sidewalk and stretched around the block. Presidents of national banks stood together with union officials, store clerks, aging golf buffs—the renowned shoulder to shoulder with the anonymous. The lieutenant-governor arrived with escort and equerry and representatives from all levels of government were sprinkled through the crowd. There were some 2,000 present. It was a display worthy of a major political leader, a film star or at least someone who had made a lot of headlines. But many curious passers-by, on asking what personage had commanded such an honour, would be little the wiser when given the name, "Tong Louie."

Tong Louie was, by the time he died, one of the leading industrialists in western Canada, one of its most active philanthropists, and a patriarch of one of its pioneering social groups, but with the modesty that was his defining characteristic, he claimed little public attention for any of this. The people who turned out to make their farewells were not there because they wanted to see or be seen. You had only to listen to the subdued exchanges along the sidewalk to realize most of these people were there because Tong Louie had meant something to them personally. He had touched them, not through the media, but in their own lives. This was a spontaneous display of affection, respect and shared sadness.

The service also bore a personal stamp. The ceremonies took the usual church form, showing typical deference to community sensibilities. There were musical interludes, first by members of the Vancouver Symphony, then by a choral group formed from the ranks of his employees who performed "Bring Him Home" and "Old Man River." Tong did his civic duty by writing cheques to the symphony orchestra, but true to his unpretentious nature, he reserved his real enthusiasm for musical theatre. As mourners left the church they were handed a small package containing a coin and a candy, a traditional gesture to thank guests for coming.

I had come to know Tong about 15 years earlier. At that time I was handling corporate relations for the Bank of BC and other Vancouver companies, earning a decent living but dreaming of someday getting back to my first love as a writer of books. We had met through my brother Ray Perrault, who was Senate House Leader at the time, and I guess I must have struck him as someone he could talk to because it wasn't long after that he invited me to meet him at the old Spanish Grill in the Hotel Vancouver to discuss a delicate piece of business. He had started sweeping floors after school in his father's wholesale grocery business, H.Y. Louie Co. Ltd., when the firm had only a handful of employees. For years the company had thrived in a close-knit family atmosphere. As merchandise manager, salesman, then CEO, Tong always managed to get to know his employees in the normal course of business and to provide leadership through informal contact. Now, more than 50 years later, the company had 3,000 employees and Tong was having trouble keeping track. He saw that if he wanted to maintain contact with his employees he had to do something of a structured nature, and he wondered if I could help him. He wasn't concerned about public recognition, but he wanted his people to know who he was, what he believed in and what he would do for them. He did not want his organization to be faceless.

TONG POSES IN FRONT OF THE HEAD OFFICE OF LONDON DRUGS IN RICHMOND.

This was right up my alley because I'd always advised my clients to "put a face on your business. Let people know who you are and what you're about." I suggested a strategy to expose him more to his people. He put the plan into practice with things like efficiency awards, programs and events where he would have a chance to mingle with and address his employees. He must have been satisfied with the results because we became good friends and kept up a working relationship until the end of his life. He used to drop in to my office as often as once a week.

It was in 1995, three years before he died, that he broached the idea of my helping him write a book about his life. His friends and colleagues had been urging him to do something like this. I leapt at the chance, and we began to have regular sessions to work on it. These would usually begin with his asking me how I was progressing and if I was nearing completion. I had to point out that since there was so little information about him and his family, I could only write a book if he gave me the material himself, which he was initially very reluctant to do. He would sit across from me, sucking on his ever-present pipe, returning my best questions with the one-word answers of the instinctively modest man who thinks anything in the world is a more worthy topic for discussion than himself. This habit was so ingrained in him I don't believe he knew how to talk about himself, effusive and amusing as he was on other topics like sports, business and current events. To make matters worse, his self-effacement affected my ability to get at people around him. He cringed at the thought of me taking up the time of respected relatives or business associates for no better reason than to discuss himself. Some he never did let me talk to.

I don't mean to give the impression he was shy, because he wasn't. At cocktail parties he would walk up to anybody in the room, glad-handing and saying, "Hi, I'm Tong Louie." He liked to disarm people by making

light of himself. Remembering him in the BC Legislature, then Health Minister Joy McPhail recalled sharing a platform with Tong to dedicate some facility he had funded. "Is there anything you want me to mention?" she asked the owner of the London Drugs store chain before stepping up to the mike. "Make sure you tell them they can get one-hour photo processing," he replied.

He was very good-humoured and he had a winning way of showing genuine interest in others. It was just himself he discounted. There was a cultural element to this, of course. Personal disclosure is not a common Chinese trait, and much as you tended to

TONG ENJOYS SOME SURF AND SUN ON ONE OF HIS RARE VACATIONS.

IN HIS FIFTIES TONG TOOK UP SALMON FISHING, ONE OF HIS FEW LEISURE ACTIVITIES.

lose sight of it, Tong was shaped by the culture of his parents in fundamental ways.

Months passed before it began to dawn on him there would be no book unless he started giving me more material, and he slowly opened up. Even after three years of hard digging I had the makings of only a small book, but family members expressed surprise I'd been able to get that much, saying they learned things about Tong and the Louie family from my manuscript that they'd never known themselves.

It is common for biographers to become disillusioned with their subjects once they have the chance to delve behind the scenes and discover the inconsistencies and misrepresentations propping up the public image, but one thing that never changed was my regard for the man himself. I was troubled from the start by the sense that he was too good to be true, and readers would not find him believable. To counter this, I made a point of pressing people I interviewed to rack their brains for anything bad they knew about him, any even faint hints of a darker side. It is hard to point up a man's qualities if you have no shadows for contrast. With a few minor exceptions that are all included in the following pages, I came up empty-handed. To those readers who will be disappointed I offer my apologies, but I did my best.

There may have been a lack of dramatic shadowing in Tong's sunshine, but that did not mean that he was either bland or dull. Effectively as he was able to hide it under his affable, ordinary guy exterior, he had the spark of genius. In his uniquely independent way, he was the chief architect of one of British Columbia's most remarkable business empires. In 1999, H.Y. Louie Co. Limited and London Drugs Limited, his two main enterprises, employed 9,000 people, making them larger than Weyerhaeuser, BC's largest forest company and second only to the Jim Pattison Group among BC-owned corporations. Even those who claim to be unmoved by such enterprise have to

TONG AND HIS WIFE GERALDINE AT
THE UNIVERSITY OF BRITISH
COLUMBIA TO ACCEPT TONG'S
HONORARY DOCTORATE OF LAWS
DEGREE IN 1989.

acknowledge the talent it takes to achieve such a thing. The dimensions of the accomplishment expand immeasurably when one considers the disadvantages Tong Louie and his brothers overcame along the way, starting from an inner city ghetto living in two rooms shared by a family of 13, and struggling every step up the ladder carrying a heavy burden of racial discrimination.

The achievement of Tong Louie goes beyond his success in business, brilliant as that was. In his low-key but boldly visionary way, he did as much as any person to gain entry for Chinese Canadians into the social and economic mainstream. He was not the only Chinese Canadian engaged in pushing back the walls of intolerance, but he did it at a crucial time and he carried it to an extraordinary level. As Roy Mah, former publisher of the *Chinatown News*, has said, "Tong blazed the way for future generations to follow."

This, then, is the story of an unsung hero most Canadians didn't know they had.

CHAPTER 1

Going to Gold Mountain

Tong Louie was a second-generation Canadian who spent his whole life in Vancouver, lived in a middle-class neighbourhood, took his family on car trips in his '57 Chevy, jogged in Stanley Park, played golf and generally lived the life of a typical city businessman. He spoke English clearly and many who had dealings with him might have been forgiven for thinking his Chinese ancestry had not played an important part in his life.

Nothing could be further from the truth.

Tong was active in the Vancouver Chinese community and took pride in his position as a member of one of Chinatown's pioneer families. His family history shaped him in two fundamental ways. First, it connected him to a rich heritage filtered down to him through his parents and through the ethnic enclave in which he spent his childhood. Second, growing up as part of any visible minority in early twentieth-century British Columbia was bound to mark a person in some way. Chinese Canadians were singled out for a particularly harsh brand of discrimination that cast its shadow over everything they did. Some people who survived this era were broken and embittered. Some learned a deep and resigned kind of tolerance. Others saw in it a challenge to improve their corner of the world to the benefit of all. This was Tong Louie's response, but it was one he inherited from his father, Hok Yat Louie, a remarkable man who established the Louie family during this very difficult time and founded the family business. Because his place is so central in Tong's story and so fascinating in its own right, it is worth looking into in some detail.

Hok Yat Louie was born in early 1875 in Doo Tow, a small village near Guangzhou (Canton), in the broad delta of the Zhu Jiang (Pearl River), some 145 kilometres inland from Hong Kong. He was the youngest of four children, with two older sisters and an older brother. His father, Doe Soong, had left for Australia when he was very young, intending to work and send back money, but very little ever materialized and his mother had to raise the family largely on her own. She couldn't afford the $2 a year to send Hok Yat to school, so he studied at night by the light of an oil lamp. By day he worked in the rice fields, earning $3 a month.

OPPOSITE: HOK YAT LOUIE CAME TO CANADA AT THE END OF THE 19TH CENTURY WITH THE DREAM OF BUILDING A BETTER FUTURE FOR HIMSELF, HIS FAMILY AND HIS DESCENDANTS.

PAGE 19: LIKE HOK YAT LOUIE, MOST OF THE EARLY CHINESE WHO CAME TO BRITISH COLUMBIA WERE POOR PEASANTS FROM THE PEARL RIVER DELTA IN GUANGDONG PROVINCE. THEY ENDURED SQUALID CONDITIONS ABOARD SHIP.

In 1894 Hok Yat entered into an arranged marriage with a young woman of the surname Kwok from the nearby village of Jook Sow Yen. They had two girls and one boy.

Most of Canada's early Chinese settlers came from the Pearl River delta, and there were reasons for it. The majority of the people were peasant farmers trapped in the grip of a centuries-old feudal system. The Manchu Dynasty (1644–1912), the last of China's great imperial dynasties, was in final decline under Emperor Kuang Hsu, though the power behind the throne was his aunt, the formidable dowager empress T'zu Hsi. The delta land was fertile but nature was unpredictable at best, visiting them with devastating floods, droughts, typhoons and blight. Mandarins taxed them; bandits harassed them; rebellions and internecine wars drained what few resources they had, and refugees from worse-off parts of the country kept crowding in on them, posing the threat of mass starvation. By 1850, the population of surrounding

ENGRAVING DEPICTS THE LAUNCH OF THE *NORTH WEST AMERICA*, THE FIRST SHIP BUILT IN BC, AT NOOTKA, 1878. IT WAS BUILT WITH THE HELP OF CHINESE CRAFTSMEN FROM THE PEARL RIVER DELTA, WHO CAME TO VANCOUVER ISLAND TO ASSIST BRITISH TRADERS IN ESTABLISHING A FORT.

THOUSANDS OF CHINESE
LABOURERS WERE BROUGHT
TO CANADA IN THE EARLY 1880S
TO HELP BUILD THE CANADIAN
PACIFIC RAILWAY.

Guangzhou had been one of the first Chinese ports opened to foreign trade, starting as a base for the British East India Company in 1694. This gave people of the delta a greater awareness of the outside world and made them especially attentive to rumours of opportunities in faraway lands where a man could elevate his family above a bare subsistence level. By the mid-nineteenth century, stories circulated widely of gold rushes in Australia, California and British Columbia, of mass hiring for a railroad crossing Canada, and work and business opportunities in places like Australia, South Africa, India and the South Pacific. North America came to be known in Chinese folklore as "Gold Mountain" because of its supposedly fabulous riches.

The lure of foreign prospects in distant lands launched a voluntary exodus of males from Guangdong province to virtually every corner of the earth. In the villages of the Pearl River delta there was a well-established tradition for looking after a man's immediate family while he was working overseas as long as he sent home all the money he could. When he reached his early twenties, Hok Yat Louie decided to join the exodus. His brother had chosen to try his luck in Australia; Hok Yat opted to head for Canada. By this time it was well known that working in Canada was no sojourn in paradise.

By 1896, Guangzhou and the territory that became British Columbia had been in contact for 100 years and possibly longer. Shadowy records exist suggesting a missionary named Hui Shen travelled down the North American coast in the late fifth century, and a booming trade in sea-otter furs started up between Guangzhou and Vancouver Island in 1785. British trading vessels began transporting Chinese workers back to Nootka Sound to help construct installations including the first sea-going ship built in the new territory, the *North West America*. It is not recorded what became of the approximately 120 Chinese workers at

Guangdong province had soared to 28 million. Nearly one million delta people lost their lives in regional wars, and 150,000 others in local battles over land and water. Some 20 million in southern and central China died during the Taiping Rebellion, which ended a few years before Hok Yat was born. The disastrous Boxer Rebellion was already being fomented with the tacit approval of the dowager empress in the hope of countering foreign influence, and would plunge the country into violence in 1900.

Nootka when the fort was abandoned some years later, but if it is true that some stayed on, they would qualify as British Columbia's first non-aboriginal settlers. In 1858 gold was discovered on the Fraser River and some Chinese who had been part of the 1849 California gold rush joined the northward stampede to the new discovery. Word spread, and the first comers were soon joined by others. By 1863, an estimated 4,000 Chinese were in the Cariboo region alone. Many spent their time searching for gold, particularly in claims abandoned by white miners, but others started up businesses as market gardeners, laundry men and cooks. Two of Vancouver's original businesses in the days when it was still called Gastown were a store run by Gin Tei Hing and a laundry run by Wah Chong. Although they did important work in all parts of the province, the Chinese were not made welcome. A fellow miner remarked, "It is the fashion on the Pacific Coast to abuse and ill-treat the Chinaman in every possible way; and I really must tell my friends [that] . . . they are hard-working, sober and law-abiding—three scarce qualities among people in the station."

When the gold rush subsided, the Chinese drifted back to urban centres where their comparatively large numbers aroused fear and hostility among white settlers. John Robson, the future BC premier, said of his Chinese neighbours, "I consider their habits as filthy as their morals, in both eating, drinking and sleeping. They sleep in beds not fit for dogs and live in dirty hovels, so how can they be clean at all?" In 1875, the new province of British Columbia formally outlawed citizens of Chinese ancestry from voting in elections, removing a right that would not be returned until 1947. At a social and economic disadvantage, many took the most dangerous and difficult jobs in the province—stringing telegraph lines through the wilderness, carving wagon roads along sheer river canyons and working in the disaster-prone coal mines of Vancouver Island. Between jobs they squatted in wilderness hovels, moved into shantytowns like the

CHINESE PLACER MINERS SLUICE FOR GOLD NEAR NORTH BEND, BC. GOLD RUSHES ON THE FRASER RIVER AND IN THE CARIBOO REGION BROUGHT MANY CHINESE TO BC IN THE 1850S AND 1860S.

one outside Cumberland, or sought the larger Chinatowns of Vancouver and Victoria where they enjoyed some sense of belonging.

Then construction began on the Canadian Pacific Railway (CPR) and suddenly they were wanted again—but only for the work they could do. Canadian Prime Minister John A. Macdonald made this clear when explaining his decision to ease immigration policy temporarily:"I share very much the feeling of the people of the United States and the Australian colonies against a Mongolian or Chinese population in our country as permanent settlers. I believe it is an alien race in every sense, that would not and could not be expected to assimilate with our Aryan population…(However) it is simply a question of alternatives—either you must have this labour or you cannot have the railway."

Andrew Onderdonk, the contractor in charge of building the westernmost section of rail, received permission to bring labourers directly from China. Between 1881 and 1884, over 15,000 Chinese entered Victoria. It is said that one Chinese worker died for every mile of railroad track they laid down. Their muscle, skill and endurance were crucial in getting the job done, but when the work ended, the railway company and the Canadian government broke their promise to pay workers their way back home, leaving them to fend for themselves wherever they were when work ended. Many found their way home or into the US but thousands were stranded unexpectedly in a raw new land where, once again, there wasn't enough work to go around and they were not wanted. To add insult to injury, in 1885 the federal government imposed a head tax of $50 on all new Chinese immigrants and rescinded the right of Chinese to vote in federal elections.

This time around there were a great many more displaced Chinese workmen than after the gold rush—some 20,000, 85 percent of whom settled in BC—a considerable mass for such a young society to

IT HAS BEEN SAID THAT ONE CHINESE WORKER DIED FOR EVERY MILE OF CPR TRACK LAID.

absorb. Some stayed in the rural areas where they were laid off, working at odd jobs. Unobtrusive shantytowns appeared behind almost every BC community. Some Chinese returned to old gold workings along the Fraser where they continued to squat in riverside hovels and sift the thinning gravel for another half-century. Most gravitated back to BC's few cities and towns where they competed for any jobs they could get.

When the Chinese statesman Liang Ch'i-ch'ao visited BC some years later he estimated there were 5,000 Chinese residents in Victoria, 1,000 in New Westminster, 500 in Nanaimo, 1,000 in the Cariboo, 4,000 in Vancouver, 1,000 in Port Alberni, and 3,000 elsewhere. Employers took advantage of the predicament by putting them to work in the salmon canning, forestry and mining industries at wages far below going rates. This in turn excited the opposition of displaced white workers, whose organizations began seeking measures to exclude or expel Asians from the workforce. Hostilities broke out in 1887 when a mob of about 300 white men attacked the camp of a Chinese land-clearing crew in Coal Harbour, the first organized violence against Chinese in Canada. The Chinese Benevolent Association, which was formed in 1884 to give Chinese a collective voice, began to fear Canada would follow other Western nations in banning Chinese immigration altogether, and in 1899 began pressing for a voluntary reduction.

It was in this inauspicious period that Hok Yat made his move. From listening to the stories of returning Chinese, he must have known what kind of reception he could expect in Canada, but like others who went before him, the prospects overseas still looked better than those at home. The United States had given in to its own anti-Chinese lobby by passing the Chinese Exclusion Act of 1882, which banned all Chinese immigration, and most other likely destinations, such as Natal and Australia, had introduced harsh restrictions on immigration, so Canada was one

ALTHOUGH THEY HAD BEEN PROMISED RETURN FARE TO CHINA, LABOURERS WERE LEFT TO FEND FOR THEMSELVES WHEREVER THEY WERE WHEN RAILROAD CONSTRUCTION ENDED.

LI HUNG CHANG, A CHINESE
STATESMAN, WAS GREETED WITH
POMP AND CEREMONY AT THE **CPR**
DOCK IN SEPTEMBER, 1896.

of the few choices left among Western nations. In 1896, with the help of family and sponsors, Hok Yat put together a bundle of personal possessions, secured enough money for ship's passage, head tax and subsistence, and said farewell to his family and to Doo Tow. His part of the bargain was to find work as soon as possible after arriving in Canada and to send back as much money as he could for as long as he could. As was the custom, his wife would live in the house of his parents and care for them and her offspring.

Thousands of men left their families under the same circumstances, many never to return, or to return only in boxes of bones for burial on Chinese soil. As Liang Ch'i-ch'ao lamented, "Here you have our native land with many tens of thousands of (sections) of rich and fertile land, yet our countrymen don't have enough to eat and are forced to risk huge sums of money to make a living abroad where they are treated like cattle, horses and slaves by other races. Who can imagine anything worse!"

CHAPTER 2

Putting Down Roots

Hok Yat made his way to Hong Kong where he took passage in steerage aboard a slow freighter destined for the provincial capital of Victoria. The long voyage across the Pacific must have been a trial for a farm boy like Hok Yat, who had spent his life on land—albeit somewhat waterlogged land. He arrived in Victoria just as a smallpox epidemic was winding down and had to spend a period in quarantine awaiting examination by a doctor. Once he had medical clearance, he paid his mandatory head tax of $50 and was granted official entry into Canada. Little is recorded about his early years in BC and there are understandable discrepancies between different family accounts. Tim Louie, Tong's older brother, gives the year of Hok Yat's arrival in BC as 1898 rather than 1896.

He worked for awhile in Victoria, then took the steamer to the boom town of Vancouver. From a distance, it seemed a much likelier place for a willing young man to make his mark than the more settled and slower-growing Victoria. His eager inquiries told him that the upstart Burrard Inlet mill town known in Chinese circles as Saltwater City was chosen as the Pacific rail terminus in 1887, and since then its population had shot up to 14,000, only 3,000 shy of the longer-established capital. The fire that had flattened Vancouver 10 years earlier was already a fading memory as new construction marched inland from the waterfront, fueled by the CPR, overseas trade and the burgeoning sawmilling and salmon canning industries. As an English traveller described the general commotion: "Above all rose the increasing noise of sawing and nail-driving, the ring of the bricklayer's trowel, the stroke of the lumberer's axe, for everyone was busy, in one way or another, building up the city." The city boasted a street railway system, and 19 kilometres of interurban track joined Vancouver to New Westminster. Roads in the downtown core were in the process of being paved or, in some cases, repaved, and the city's first suburb, Mount Pleasant, had been established on the south side of False Creek. The skyline along the waterfront was dominated by the turreted bulk of the new CPR train station. Beside it, the CPR wharves had since 1891 served as home to the Empress Liners, elegant white-hulled steamers that completed the railroad's all-red route to the Orient, transporting

CHINESE WORKERS LAYING DOWN RAILS IN VANCOUVER. BY THE TIME HOK YAT LOUIE ARRIVED IN VANCOUVER, THE CITY BOASTED A STREET RAILWAY SYSTEM AND AN INTERURBAN TRACK LINKING IT TO NEW WESTMINSTER.

silk and tea as well as passengers. Farther up Granville Street at Georgia, the first Vancouver Hotel loomed over the city, with a grand verandah overlooking the inlet and its forest of sailing ship masts. A Hudson's Bay department store had gone up across from the hotel while just down the street the Vancouver Opera House seated 2,000 and featured appearances by the great stars of the day such as the actress Mrs. Patrick Campbell and the pianist Ignacy Paderewski.

Companies that would later figure prominently in Hok Yat's life had just opened their doors, including the BC Sugar Refinery, built by Benjamin Rogers,

Vancouver's first millionaire, and Woodward's dry goods store, destined to grow into one of western Canada's largest department store chains. A variety of other companies operated out of warehouses along the Burrard Inlet waterfront, including the leading grocery wholesaler, W.H. Malkin and Co. The Oppenheimer brothers, Charles, Isaac and David, had some years earlier opened a wholesale grocery business in Vancouver's first brick building, still standing in 2002 at Columbia and Powell streets. Christ Church Cathedral, completed in 1895, ministered to the city's Church of England elite, who occupied the

stately homes on Blue Blood Alley and other quality addresses on the city's west side. Ethnic populations and blue-collar workers were relegated to the Strathcona district on the industrial east side, but even their minimal comforts were not available to Hok Yat.

Chinese arriving in Saltwater City had only one option, and that was Chinatown. Centred at Pender and Carrall streets, with Cordova as its northern boundary, Chinatown was a densely inhabited six-block ghetto where it was not unusual to find 15 men sharing a single tiny dwelling. Although the city hadn't bothered connecting the shacks along Pender Street to the sewer system, the Chinese were blamed for the unsanitary results. The year of Hok Yat's arrival, a

WHEN HOK YAT FIRST SET FOOT IN VANCOUVER CIRCA 1900, ONE OF THE CITY'S MOST DISTINGUISHED LANDMARKS WAS THE ORIGINAL VANCOUVER HOTEL, LOCATED AT GRANVILLE AND GEORGIA STREETS.

A CHINESE PROCESSION IN
VANCOUVER IN 1896.

group of merchants registered a complaint with the city about the bad living conditions on Pender Street. In subsequent years they would ask the council to make a number of improvements to the area, including paving the streets and providing them with garbage pickup. When the latter wasn't done to their satisfaction, they hired someone to do the job properly for them. Despite the rough edges, a Vancouver Tourist Association was already busy promoting Chinatown as an attraction where visitors might observe "the Oriental with his plaited queue" and no less amazing, Oriental infants, those "atoms of humanity whose jet black slanting eyes are just as shiningly inquisitive as white babies." The traveller was also directed to a rice mill powered by a human treadmill and to the Chinese

theatre, animated by "a company of no mean histrionic ability" whose costumes "are handsomely and richly embroidered with gold."

Hok Yat's first and overriding concern when he arrived in Vancouver was to start making money to send home. He had few options. He had no trade and no knowledge of English, an asset that would have opened more doors for him. He also lacked connections with the small but affluent group of Chinese merchants gaining ascendancy in Chinatown. Chang Toy, Loo Gee Wing, Yip Sang and others engaged in everything from import and export to real estate to labour contracting, tantalizing hungry young men like Hok Yat with proof that material success was possible in this country, despite the discouraging outward appearances.

While Chinatown was an enclave imposed on the Chinese by the surrounding population, it was also a haven for the Chinese bachelors and new immigrants who relied heavily on each other for survival and formed into clan and village groups based on old-world affiliations. The grid of poor streets provided a refuge where they could replenish their stock of herbal medicines, get together with old friends, play a little fan-tan, perhaps visit some girls, and be free for awhile from the taunts of Occidentals. From the city's point of view, Chinatown housed a cheap labour pool that was very convenient for the sawmill and cannery operators, as well as for land developers and farmers operating in and around the city.

The one thing Hok Yat did know was how to work the soil, especially wet delta soil, so the first job he found was as a field hand on drained land along the north shore of the Fraser River. Marginal though this work was, it allowed him to feed himself while he looked for something better. Seeing that Chinese were paid barely enough to survive on and were always the first to be laid off, he quickly figured out that he wouldn't get anywhere as a labourer.

As Liang Ch'i-ch'ao described the situation, "The majority of the labourers in British Columbia get their jobs from the salmon fishery. It's been calculated that each year during the fishing season, those who work in this business can earn no less than $30 to $60 or $70 US a month. But the season only runs from May until August. As for the rest of the year, all those involved in the fishing industry are unable to find jobs. With no resources, they can only sit and eat. That is why, before the year is out, they are left with no means of sustaining themselves. Other than working in the fish canneries, the only principal forms of employment remaining are work as a cook and in a laundry. Work

CHINESE IN TRADITIONAL DRESS, REPLETE WITH BRAIDED PIGTAILS, GAVE VANCOUVER'S CHINATOWN AN EXOTIC FLAVOUR CIRCA 1900. A FLEDGLING TOURIST ASSOCIATION WAS ALREADY PROMOTING THE DISTRICT'S ATTRACTIONS.

as a cook of the very highest class can bring in $70 to $80 US a month. The lowest class only gets something over $10 a month. Laundry work pays very little. Monthly earnings probably run something over ten dollars US a month...As for the rest, there are miners, loggers and the like, but not very many."

Gang bosses and labour contractors earned a little more serving as intermediaries assembling crews for mills, mines and canneries, but again, that required a working knowledge of English. For Hok Yat, who was born carrying the entrepreneurial gene, the obvious solution was to go into business for himself, but that required at least some small portion of capital.

He compromised. Although Chinese were not allowed to buy land at this time, white farmers would lease some in exchange for clearing it. Together with two others, he leased acreage along the north bank of the Fraser River, at the foot of what is now Boundary Road, and began to farm vegetables. The men's main cash outlay was for basic shelter, seed, fertilizer, and a horse and wagon. Around the Lower Mainland, as many as 100 other Chinese farmers were doing the same thing, growing and delivering vegetables to the city.

Hok Yat immediately began demonstrating the enterprise that would raise him above the common crowd. The workload he assumed was daunting. His main responsibility was to deliver the vegetable crop to the markets in Vancouver. This meant rising at three in the morning to reach the city by seven. With the horse harnessed and the wagon loaded with produce, he started up the steep, rutted track of Kerr Road. Except for the buildings at the Stewart fruit farm, the only signs of human life he was likely to see along the way were other produce wagons. Often he startled deer and black bears as his horse plodded north toward town.

The two-mile stretch of Kerr Road ended at Westminster Road, where Hok Yat turned his horse and wagon left and began the five-mile haul to Chinatown, passing through Mount Pleasant on the way, and stopping to water his horse at Brewery Creek. Once in Chinatown, he distributed his produce among the wholesalers and a few small retail stores, fed his horse a bag of oats, and began the long trip back to his leasehold farm. There, he would unharness the horse, wash it and the wagon, and then go into the fields to help his partners with the cultivating and harvesting of vegetables. Into the night, the three men would trim and wash produce before loading it into the wagon for the next day's trip. Hok Yat was lucky to get five hours sleep a night.

The most difficult and important work he took on at this time had nothing to do with farming, though it would pay much higher dividends in the end. He had decided to teach himself English. His wagon became his self-appointed schoolroom. Equipped with a Chinese-English phrase book that matched Chinese characters to English and offered clues on pronunciation, he spent the long hours on the road attempting to wrap his tongue around English words, holding the book in one hand, the reins in the other, as his horse and wagon inched along.

The market gardening venture didn't last. Under the hot summer sun, it was difficult to keep the produce fresh during the four- to five-hour trips to market. In the winter, snow and mud made it almost impossible to deliver anything, when there was anything to deliver.

CHINATOWN WAS AS MUCH A REFUGE AS A GHETTO, A PLACE WHERE MEN COULD GO AND RELAX IN THE COMPANY OF FRIENDS IN FAMILIAR SURROUNDINGS.

Photo: James Crookall

Finally, there was the unpredictability of the Fraser River. Dikes built to retain it broke in 1894, flooding the reclaimed farmlands. The same occurred in 1898, and Hok Yat saw no reason why it wouldn't happen again. He had seen enough of this in the Pearl River delta. His first attempt at self-employment had failed.

Those long wagon trips to and from Chinatown were still about the most rewarding time he would ever spend, however, because of the English lessons. In a biographical essay Tim wrote about Hok Yat in August 2002, he lists a number of other temporary jobs including work at a sawmill on the Fraser, work at another farm near the south foot of Main Street and work in the Fraser Valley at a wheat farm owned by future BC premier John Oliver. In Tong's account, Hok Yat had gained enough fluency in English to get hired on as shift foreman at the Hastings Sawmill, Vancouver's original mill on the edge of Burrard Inlet. His natural leadership qualities combined with his growing command of English made him ideal for the job, but the months he spent there were only the means to an end. He was already planning his re-entry into private business.

Hok Yat was through with market gardening, but he'd been keeping his sharp eyes open and he thought he'd spotted a demand nobody else was filling. By 1900, there were 130 Chinese farmers around the city. They lived from hand to mouth with long periods of no income and he knew from experience that it was hard for them to get the seeds, fertilizers, chemicals and food staples they needed. With his improving command of English, his knowledge of farming and his growing circle of friends within the Chinese community, Hok Yat decided to have another stab at starting his own business.

Using money he had saved working at the sawmill, he rented a small store and started up a wholesale and retail grocery and farm supply business. Tong dates this move in 1903, although Tim places it as late as 1907 and gives the location of the store as 922 Westminster Avenue. Tong thought the first store was at Pender and Carrall, and said the Westminster location came later. In any case it was a plucky move. The wholesale food supply business was the preserve of Vancouver's wealthiest and most powerful men. Oppenheimer Bros. & Co. was directed by David Oppenheimer, Vancouver's second mayor and head of a business clique that controlled city affairs for years. William Harold Malkin of W.H. Malkin and Co. would also take his turn as mayor, and his great warehouse with its outsized rooftop sign was a waterfront

PENDER STREET WAS A BUSY PLACE IN THE MORNINGS, WHEN CHINESE FARMERS LIKE HOK YAT BROUGHT THEIR PRODUCE TO THE CITY TO SELL AMONG THE WHOLESALERS AND RETAIL STORES IN CHINATOWN.

landmark that must have been one of the first things Hok Yat saw when he viewed his new home from the deck of the Victoria steamer. Peppery little Bob Kelly and his partner Frank Douglas of Kelly Douglas Ltd. were too busy making their fortune provisioning the thousands of Klondike gold rushers pouring through BC to be bothered with local politics, and would soon erect their own waterfront landmark next to the CPR station. All of these flinty tycoons were jealous of their turf and wouldn't hesitate to scuttle even the smallest competitor, as Hok Yat would discover.

As Liang Ch'i-ch'ao assessed the situation in 1903, "Taking a look at the business situation in British Columbia (only with respect to Chinese merchants) we find there are over 140 businesses in Victoria. In Vancouver there are some 50-odd. In New Westminster there are twenty to thirty. You cannot say the number is not large. However, only one or two do business with Westerners. All the rest depend on Chinese labourers to support them." This was the crowded field Hok Yat was joining, but the idea of supplying Chinese truck farmers did give the venture a tentative foothold.

Every day was an exercise in walking a financial tightrope. For most of his supplies Hok Yat had to rely on the established wholesalers. While his command of English enabled him to deal with their representatives, he needed to win their confidence. To do this he had to pay them either in advance or precisely on time. The banks would not grant him loans, or extend credit, which placed him in a financial bind. When Hok Yat delivered planting supplies to farmers in the spring, he knew they would not be able to pay him until after harvest in mid-summer and autumn.

He did many things to bridge the gaps. Many of the inhabitants of Chinatown, and of the farmlands beyond, hailed from the four counties of the Pearl River delta and spoke dialects he could understand. Very few of them spoke or understood English and all

IN 1900 THERE WERE APPROXIMATELY 130 CHINESE-RUN FARMS IN THE VANCOUVER AREA.

WHEN H.Y. LOUIE VENTURED INTO
THE WHOLESALE FOOD BUSINESS IN
THE EARLY 1900S, THE VANCOUVER
WATERFRONT WAS DOMINATED BY
THE WAREHOUSES OF HIS MUCH
LARGER COMPETITORS, W.H.
MALKIN AND KELLY DOUGLAS,
KNOWN FOR ITS NABOB BRAND.

OPPOSITE TOP: A VIEW OF
VANCOUVER IN 1911, THE YEAR
HOK YAT MARRIED HIS SECOND
WIFE, YOUNG SHEE. HASTINGS
SAWMILL, WHERE HOK YAT WORKED
AS CREW FOREMAN CAN BE SEEN
SMOKING IN THE DISTANCE BEHIND
THE WHITE-HULLED SAILING SHIP.

of them felt the sting of discrimination. Hok Yat was a straw to reach for: he was one of their own who had demonstrated that he could handle himself in the white man's environment. He had a natural self-assurance that impressed his countrymen, and they began turning to him for advice and counsel. The Chinese mistrusted the white institutions generally, and paper currency specifically. Still, most of them had savings, no matter how small, and they were eager to get them converted to gold. Hok Yat formed a relationship with a Seattle currency dealer named Dexter Horton and through him was able to get gold for the men, charging a small percentage for his services. It was one of many sidelines that opened up to Hok Yat because of his growing reputation as an intermediary, and it helped him survive through the rocky early stages of his business.

In those start-up years, Hok Yat had a partner named Chung Yin Fong. The workload, financial pressures and the formidable task of gaining the support of suppliers took its toll on both of them. Hok Yat's days began before dawn and ended at midnight when he dropped onto his mattress at the back of the store. The brutal hours, intimidating debts and minuscule return discouraged Chung Yin Fong. It had the opposite effect on Hok Yat. He was fully aware of the difficulties, but he saw a glimmer of hope and it excited him. He was in for the long haul and refused to let anxieties of the moment cloud his thinking. He sat down with his partner and agreed on a buyout that freed Chung and transferred sole responsibility for settling debts onto his own broad back. Left to sink or swim on his own, he redoubled his efforts to keep the enterprise alive.

As Tong remembered his father's telling of events, he moved to larger premises after a couple of years (probably the building Tim placed at 922 Westminster Avenue) and changed the name of the business to the

Kwong Chong Company. Trade was improving somewhat, with an increasing number of farmers coming to him for agricultural supplies. As well, he began to cater to the restaurants, laundries and small grocery stores now multiplying in Chinatown and beyond.

He had a difficult relationship with his wholesalers and suppliers. Even though his reputation for paying his accounts was firmly established, white-owned businesses always got placed ahead of him on the priority list. Wholesalers such as BC Sugar, Kelly Douglas Ltd. and W.H. Malkin and Co. dealt with him grudgingly, and antipathy toward the Chinese was at an all time high among the general public. In 1907 a mob organized by a group called the Asiatic Exclusion League rioted through Chinatown, breaking windows and causing $25,000 damage, marking a low point in BC race relations.

According to Tim Louie's account, Hok Yat "found the location at 922 Westminster to be a little too far from Chinatown (about four blocks) and he was missing some of the action," so he moved his premises once more. At this time established Chinese merchants were negotiating mortgages, often with white-owned trust companies, or with the Chinese

merchant princes, enabling them to erect permanent buildings, usually three storeys high and made of red brick. Encouraged by these examples, Hok Yat negotiated an agreement to buy the Urquhart Building at 255 East Georgia in 1908. It was two storeys high, 25 feet wide and 120 feet long, fronted in white glazed brick and it would serve as a business address and a home for many years.

BELOW: A HYSTERICAL MOB SWEPT THROUGH CHINATOWN IN SEPTEMBER 1907, CHANTING RACIST SLOGANS, CAUSING $25,000 DAMAGE AND TERRIFYING RESIDENTS. THE NEXT DAY WINDOWS WERE BOARDED UP AND CHINESE WORKERS STAYED OFF THE JOB.

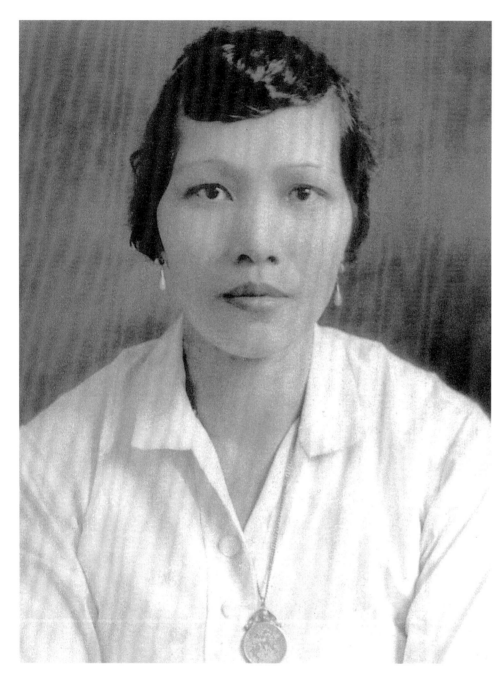

AT THE AGE OF **19**, YOUNG SHEE
LEFT CHINA TO BECOME HOK YAT
LOUIE'S BRIDE AND START A NEW
LIFE WITH HIM IN CANADA.

he could never aspire to in his homeland. Who could say, maybe in years to come the ardours of frontier life would cool, making way for a more civilized society in which his grandchildren could move about as equals. As Confucius said, "Men's natures are alike; it is their habits that carry them far apart." Habits could change over time. It was the faith Hok Yat lived by, and one he would pass on to his heirs.

But if he was going to have heirs in this country, he would have to have a wife in this country. He was now 33 and time was marching on. His first wife could not come to Canada because she was obliged by custom to stay in Doo Tow and care for his parents. From the time he arrived, he had sent her a share of his earnings and would continue to do so as long as he lived. But Chinese custom allowed a man to have more than one wife, and wealthy men like Yip Sang often had several, so Hok Yat arranged through an intermediary to search out a suitable and willing partner back home. The search settled on a 19-year-old peasant girl named Young Shee, an only child who lived with her mother in another district far from Doo Tow. They were very poor and looked upon the opportunity to marry Young Shee to an overseas Chinese as heaven-sent relief. While waiting for this to transpire, Hok Yat crossed another fateful bridge: he took out Canadian citizenship.

In 1911, Young Shee stepped ashore in Vancouver. She was met by Hok Yat, who led her into the maze of Chinatown and then through the doors of his home and warehouse at 255 East Georgia.

Two years after Young Shee arrived in Vancouver she gave birth to their first child. Much to Hok Yat's satisfaction, it was a boy. Had they been in China the whole village would have celebrated. Sons were favoured and valued. In that light, Hok Yat's record as a father was above reproach—the next six children were all boys. They named the first son Tim. Tong was born 14 months later on March 1, 1914.

Acquiring substantial new quarters was not the only thing that made this period a turning point in the struggling merchant's life. He was making some big decisions, and the biggest one was that he would stay here in Canada and cast his lot with this new country that was so hostile to his people but offered so much

CHAPTER 3

A Child of Chinatown

Tong was born at a time of great change in the world. In Western literature, critics pinpoint 1914 as the year in which the modern period began. An epochal shift was in the offing. The previous year, Henry Ford had introduced production line manufacturing at his Detroit automobile plant, a move that would eventually put 15 million Model Ts on the road and bring an end to the days of horse and buggy. Some 500 jitneys, privately owned Model Ts that picked up passengers ahead of the streetcars, would soon be competing with Vancouver's 160 streetcars. It was only four months since US President Woodrow Wilson pushed the button that opened the Panama Canal, moving Vancouver 6,000 sea miles closer to Europe and the Eastern Seaboard. News was still filtering down about Thomas Edison's latest invention, a device called the "kinetophone," which produced talking motion pictures. It would be nine months before Alexander Graham Bell picked up a phone in New York and dialed his assistant in San Francisco, completing the first transcontinental telephone call. Most of the technological advances that would change twentieth-century life beyond the wildest imaginings

of previous generations were just beginning to be talked about by ordinary people.

On the political front too, it was a time that would change the world beyond recognition. In China, it was two years since the last emperor, six-year-old Pu-yi, abdicated the imperial throne, ending dynastic rule that stretched back 5,000 years. The revolutionary group led by Dr. Sun Yat-sen was now trying to reshape the country into a modern republic. And it was only four months before Europe would plunge the world into the most devastating war in history.

On the home front, the business boom that Vancouver had been riding since the depression of the 1890s, with only a short reversal in 1907, finally crashed to earth in the nasty depression of 1913. The city population would experience its biggest drop ever as a total of 55,000 British Columbians shipped overseas to do battle in Europe's rat-infested trenches. It was a bad time for Vancouver's Chinese population, in spite of its efforts to ingratiate itself with the white community. A couple of years earlier, in preparation for the Duke of Connaught's official visit, the Chinese decorated their crowded quarter and erected an ornate

QUAN AND ERNIE. FROM AN EARLY AGE THE LOUIE BOYS WERE KEPT BUSY DOING CHORES IN THE FAMILY BUSINESS.

歡迎

WELCOME

THIS IMPOSING ARCH WAS ERECTED AT THE ENTRANCE TO CHINATOWN TO WELCOME THE DUKE OF CONNAUGHT TO VANCOUVER IN 1912. INTENDED AS A GESTURE OF GOODWILL AND LOYALTY, IT WAS RIDICULED IN THE WHITE PRESS AS DISTASTEFUL AND PRESUMPTUOUS.

arch that spanned the width of Pender Street at the entrance to Chinatown. The idea was to show allegiance to Canada and the British monarch, but it backfired. Vancouver's white establishment, far from feeling complimented, couldn't contain its indignation, denouncing the well-meant demonstration as presumptuous and in bad taste. To bewildered leaders of the Chinese community, it seemed they couldn't win.

While the war effort pressed large numbers of white women into industrial work for the first time, employment for the Chinese bottomed out. At one point during the war, unemployment rose to 80 percent among BC Chinese, prompting the Chinese Benevolent Association to again advise people of the Pearl River delta to stay where they were. "Dear uncles and brothers," their circular began, "the Association (is) advising our fellow countrymen to refrain from coming to Canada . . . innumerable overseas Chinese are jobless and many are suffering from cold and hunger. They are so miserable their anguish is beyond description."

As if this weren't enough, municipal and provincial governments found time to impose further restrictions. Chinese grocers were discouraged from locating outside Chinatown and were charged much more for business licences than white grocers. Health inspectors closed them down for the slightest breach, real or imaginary, and white farmers lobbied to prevent the Chinese from owning or leasing farmland. Provincial regulations were passed banning Chinese from working on government projects or in underground mines. These petty strictures contributed to hopelessness and hunger. In Chinatown, the Chinese Salvation and Welfare Committee and the Chinese United Association organized to provide free meals and accommodation for the destitute.

Thanks to his independent business and the food he had stored in his warehouse, Hok Yat was able to weather these bad times, supporting his growing family without having to turn to charity. He devoted what time he could spare to helping the less fortunate, sometimes giving out food, or helping people find work.

Tong was too young to recall much about the war years. He remembered the dense fogs that enveloped the entire town in the fall and winter, but didn't know at the time that they were caused by smoke belching from beehive sawdust burners at the many sawmills lining the shores of False Creek and Burrard Inlet. Overnight, shipbuilding had become the city's largest industry, employing 5,000, and a wartime shipyard on False Creek made its own contribution to the smothering curtain that obscured the streets.

As Alan Morley wrote in *Vancouver: From Milltown to Metropolis*, the First World War had an impact on the city that is difficult for later generations to appreciate. "Much more than the Second World War, it was an intensely personal conflict to the people of Vancouver. Canada's casualties in 1914–1918 were greater than those of the entire United States forces. There were streets in Vancouver where every house had a man overseas, and in which every block mourned its two or three dead before the armistice came. For sheer, grinding merciless slaughter, the Hitler War never approached it."

Some of the most profound changes wrought by World War I took place far from the battlefield. Wars have always been catalysts of change, but more change was poised to happen in 1914 than ever in the past. Before the war, airplanes were still considered a rare curiosity of no practical interest; afterward, war surplus Tiger Moths, "Jennies" and Curtiss Flying Boats were barnstorming, bush flying and carrying mail in every direction, flown by a battalion of war-trained pilots. The same was true of the thousand technological advances in countless fields.

Equally profound was the sea change in social attitudes. The war left Canada a sadder and wiser country. It also shook up inflexible Victorian Age attitudes about religion, morality and class and delivered Canadians into a new age where, as Albert Einstein postulated in 1905, everything was relative. Old systems were in flux. The Jazz Age was dawning. Women were bobbing their hair and exposing their ankles, even their calves. For people of Tong's age, who came to awareness in this post-war period, it meant the generational gulf that separated them from their parents, already wide enough, would become wider still.

Despite its own wartime difficulties, the Chinese community kept up its traditional festivities, bringing delight to the children and respite to the adults. Tong remembered the Festival of the Lunar Year, with its bright display of fireworks, the cavorting of the lion and dragon dancers, and the serving of treats hoarded for the occasion. He also recalled trips to Stanley Park with his mother and some of his brothers, though never with his father. Young Shee was a gentle and

patient person, capable of influencing her husband in domestic matters, but quite detached from his business, both by custom and by choice. As a mother in the Chinese tradition, her principal role was to bear children and see to their health and welfare, as well as that of her husband. She bore eleven children and her husband delivered every one of them himself in the stark surroundings of their upstairs rooms. At first they couldn't afford a doctor and Vancouver's hospitals did little to encourage the Chinese to attend them—one even segregated Chinese patients in the basement. In any case, most Chinese people of that generation had little use for Western medicine and tending to their own home births was the least of their problems. After Tong came Bill, Ernie, Quan, John, Edward, Helen, Beatrice, Willis, and finally in 1932, Ken.

There was no such thing as privacy in the small space above the family business. Tong remembered his mother's pregnancies, and his father sending him to the other end of the building, or out into the streets, when he delivered the current offspring. On one occasion, the birth was particularly difficult. Tong never forgot his mother's distress and the copious amount of blood following the birth. Her periods of recovery were brief; within a day or two she would be back to housekeeping, nursing the new infant as she went about her duties.

Hok Yat was a different kind of parent, patriarchal to a fault, intensely focussed on establishing himself and providing for his family, but showing few outward signs of affection. One of Tong's earliest memories of his father was from behind his mother's skirts as she fended off Hok Yat's angry attempts to give him a licking. He didn't remember the cause, but felt he probably deserved it. His father was a stern provider, was there for them when they needed him, and taught by example.

When Tong was eight, Hok Yat showed him how to fill out an invoice.

HOK YAT HAD THIS PORTRAIT TAKEN OF HIS ENTIRE 13-MEMBER FAMILY SHORTLY BEFORE HE EMBARKED ON HIS LONG-DELAYED VISIT TO CHINA. BACK ROW: TONG (B.1914), TIM (1913), ERNIE (1918) AND BILL (1916); MIDDLE ROW, QUAN (1921), YOUNG SHEE HOLDING KENNY (1932), HELEN (1925), HOK YAT, JOHN (1922) AND BEATRICE (1928); FRONT ROW, EDDIE (1923) AND WILLIS (1930).

WILLIS LOUIE RECEIVES A
HOLLYWOOD BUSS FROM HIS OLDER
SISTER BEATRICE. WITH BOTH
PARENTS FULLY OCCUPIED, THE 11
LOUIE CHILDREN MADE UP THEIR
OWN ENTERTAINMENT.

Tong was four when the war ended and from that time forward his memories were better. He clearly remembered the details of his family's living quarters. There were three partitioned spaces, all without doors, serving as kitchen and sleeping areas. Sanitary arrangements were rudimentary and, for the first years, there was no electricity. Tim, in his short history of his father written in August 2002, adds a few more details: "There was a mezzanine style floor used as a bedroom. The main floor kitchen, wash basin, toilet and cooking stove were all in the same cramped quarters. The hot water didn't work too well so you would have to heat your own water in a pot-belly cast iron kettle if you wished to take a bath. This was where we all lived and grew up until 1930, when father had a new building constructed at 254 East Georgia with a proper modern kitchen and bath-room." But even at the old place the roof didn't leak, there was food on the table and mattresses to sleep on. For a small boy like Tong, who'd never known dif-ferent, it might just as well have been the Imperial Palace.

雷滔

雷學溢限有公司

YOUNG SHEE LOUIE WITH
DAUGHTERS BEATRICE AND HELEN
IN FRONT OF THE H.Y. LOUIE CO.
LTD. WAREHOUSE AT 255 EAST
GEORGIA STREET. FOR YEARS THE
GROWING FAMILY LIVED IN THE
CRAMPED UPPER ROOMS OF THE
BUILDING.

Tong's early explorations were limited to Chinatown, with False Creek as the southern boundary and Hastings Street on the north. Chinese parents were all too conscious of the hostile forces that lurked outside their familiar streets and wanted to protect the young ones as long as they could. Fortunately for Tong, life within these confines was far from boring. For a start, there were the streets and alleys of Chinatown to explore. Here the architecture of the better structures resembled those of towns in the Pearl River delta; red brick, seldom more than three storeys high, with recessed balconies and ornate, wrought iron railings. Almost all of them housed a business at the street level, with a living area and storage facilities on the floor above.

Chinese herbalist shops exuded odours that mingled with the scents from restaurants and steam wafting from the laundries. Although Western clothes were slowly coming into style and the once-ubiquitous pigtail had vanished, many people bustled along the walkways in flat-soled shoes and loose-fitting Chinese clothing. Along the streets the hubbub of voices, the rumble of cartwheels and the clatter of the dray horses blended with the muffled rattle of mahjong pieces tumbling on the tables of the gambling rooms and the strains of Chinese instruments. To the residents, this was the known and familiar part of the world, for all that it seemed mysterious and menacing to outsiders. Sax Rohmer's novels about the sinister character Dr. Fu Manchu had infected the public imagination with images of hatchet men, opium dens and white slave traders, making Chinatown seem as threatening in the eyes of white parents as it was comforting in the eyes of Chinese ones.

Out on Hastings Street at the outer limits of Tong's home territory, the scene changed, and Tong would only dare to explore it as he got bigger. The city hall and impressive new Carnegie Library, with its ornamental rough-cut stone walls and arresting dome, dominated the area and marked the transition to the outside world. The sidewalk traffic was mostly Occidental, mixed with Chinese, Japanese and Indo-Canadians there on business. Chinese women were rarely seen in public, but a few brave housewives emerged to shop at Woodward's new emporium where, on "95-Cent Day" you could buy anything from a cotton dress to a canning pot for 95 cents.

The five-block stretch west along Hastings was a circus of activity. The bulging eyes of red snappers stared from beds of crushed ice in the window of the Only Seafood Restaurant; shoemakers worked over their lasts at the Pierre Paris boot store, favoured by loggers looking for the best in caulk-studded boots; penny treasures radiated temptation from the counters of the five-and-ten-cent store.

The usual passing parade was fascinating enough, but when the woods closed down because of

LOUIE YOUNGSTERS JOHN, ED, HELEN AND QUAN PLAY A GAME OF MARBLES.

forest fires or winter snows, the loggers came to town. They filled the hotels and rooming houses in the skid row district, and overflowed onto Hastings Street. Here, tattoo artists demonstrated their skill in kiosks set up on the sidewalk; lady barbers sat their clients on chairs and sheared hair in full view of the public; street hawkers sold miracle cures side by side with evangelists warning sinners to return to the fold before the end of the world caught them unprepared. Some days the Salvation Army band marched to a street corner, formed a circle and pounded out a concert of dissonant hymns while a few more comely soldiers of the cross worked the crowd with upturned tambourines. Loggers in their cups could be generous, and they were in their cups as often as they could arrange it. During the war years, Prohibition was in effect, but the lumberjacks and other wayfarers could

always find a bootlegger. Tong learned to give them a wide berth.

There was the cenotaph at Victory Square to be inspected, and another war memorial in front of the CPR station where a bronze soldier was being hoisted to his reward in the arms of a ministering angel. Young Tong could lean on the railing and gaze down across the rail yards to the sparkling waters of Burrard Inlet, where steamers and the occasional sailing ship eased their way into berth and the North Vancouver ferry performed its interminable shuttle.

On rainy days, if his father's plans didn't restrict him to chores around the store, he could escape to the library where several floors of books shared space with a small museum. He was fascinated by the museum's prize exhibit, the mummified remains of an Egyptian boy, whose leathery little face carried such an expressive

grimace down through the ages. Tong felt a pang of empathy and took to paying him regular visits, like a favourite relative confined to hospital. While there he would linger over the murderous-looking collection of barbed spears from New Guinea, the musty old Indian blankets from the Queen Charlotte Islands, Spanish cannon balls and the intricate ceramics, embroidered silk robes, and bronze artifacts from China. Here, for the first time, he saw works of his own culture displayed side by side with treasures from Greece and Rome, as if all were equal in the eyes of science. It was a revelation to him. When he learned to read, he realized the library was where the real treasures were, and it became an even more important force in his life than the museum. He would never forget what the library had meant to him, and decades later he would repay the debt.

In good weather he could play with his brothers and sisters or find friends among the children of other Chinese families whose parents were busy working in their downstairs businesses. Left to their own devices,

the kids invented their own amusements. There were minnows and crabs to be caught along the shores of False Creek. All of them were addicted to the games of the day: marbles, peggy, kick-the-can. If there were enough of them, they could start pickup games of soccer and baseball on the False Creek flats, or any cleared area they could find that was not out of bounds. Even at an early age Tong was good at sports. One of his regrets was that he couldn't have participated more, but he didn't have time.

His weekday routine was crowded. In addition to attendance at public school, he and his siblings went to Chinese school. When the public school day ended at three in the afternoon, they walked to the Chinese school at 460 Keefer Street where, from five o'clock on they studied Cantonese reading, writing and conversation, as well as Chinese history and culture. Most of the students already knew each other from playing together on the streets of Chinatown, but one face that wasn't familiar was that of a pretty little girl whose parents lived in the city's West End. Her parents were among the few Chinese of that time who lived in a white neighbourhood and enjoyed the respect of their neighbours. Her father was an agent for the CPR and a well-known figure around the city, as well as a director of the school. She was very Canadian in her manner, but at the same time very knowledgeable about Chinese culture. She was four years younger than Tong and he would have scoffed at the thought she could ever mean anything to him, but their paths would cross again. Her name was Maysien Geraldine Seto. The Chinese language schools were the only places the children of the city's Chinese residents met as a distinct group, and many lifelong friendships were formed. The sessions at the Keefer Street school could last from two to three hours, after which Tong returned to the family quarters for supper, followed by homework and chores.

Tong's day ended in the dark space where he and his siblings slept. Beyond the partition the latest baby whimpered and was consoled by the low voice of his mother. The great spotlight circling the sky above the roof of Woodward's department store shot intermittent beams of light through the small window while below, among the bags, barrels and boxes in the store, Hok Yat Louie worked into the wee hours preparing for the next day's trade.

Sundays at the Louie habitation were meeting days for the men's group Hok Yat cultivated. Chinatown residents were compulsive formers of associations. By the time the 1920s began, there were at least 20 clan associations, and half again as many home district organizations. They were support groups for their members and some wielded considerable power within Chinatown's confines. Today we would call it networking. Chinese called it guanxi (pronounced guan shee.) To get things done requires guanxi. You scratch my back, I scratch yours. Hok Yat, showing the independence of mind that marked everything he did,

apparently decided to work a variation on the traditional Chinese social structure by starting a group of his own that would offer some of the benefits of the others but carry fewer of the commitments. It was an informal collection whose unifying tie was the members' acquaintance with Hok Yat, who served as their mentor, giving them advice on their finances and business matters and sometimes even lending them money. Often, he acted as judge and mediator when arguments and altercations occurred. Those he helped became friends and customers. There is no indication that he had trouble with the clans or home district organizations, or that he was in competition with them in any way. Compared to Chinatown's merchant princes, he was a small cog in the wheel. The little group surrounding him might be called a voluntary association, a symbiotic arrangement that would assist him and his growing family in the difficult days ahead. On one level it can only be understood in terms of the old-world tradition it grew out of; on another it was simply a matter of recognizing people as the ultimate resource, which is good business in any culture. In time Tong would learn the art of cultivating relationships from his father and carry it to new heights, but for now it was understood that during these Sunday sessions children were not to be seen or heard. Tong and the others hit the street.

As for Young Shee, her series of pregnancies, the unending routine of shopping, cooking, sewing, and cleaning for her steadily expanding family left her with very little time for recreation. She still sometimes took her children on outings to Stanley Park and the public beaches, travelling by streetcar. Occasionally she took them to performances of Chinese theatre and opera, but she rarely sat with them at the five-cent movie matinees in theatres along Hastings Street as she couldn't understand the dialogue. She spent most of her time at home or on domestic missions on the streets of Chinatown.

ALL THE LOUIE CHILDREN
ATTENDED STRATHCONA
ELEMENTARY SCHOOL ON
EAST PENDER STREET.

Tong and his 10 siblings all attended Strathcona School. Strathcona was nicknamed the League of Nations and it lived up to the billing. Japanese were in the majority, but in the early twenties about a quarter of the student body was Chinese, with a good showing by Jews, Ukrainians, Scandinavians, blacks and a smattering of others, including Gypsies.

Tong's father, knowing how valuable his own limited education had been, took his children's schooling seriously. His stern advice was to keep clean, study hard and walk away from racial challenges when playing with white children. As with most Pearl River delta people, Hok Yat Louie was infused with Confucian

values that led him to practise patience, bide his time and bite his tongue in the presence of discrimination and injustice. He directed his children to do the same. It was advice Tong took to heart, and it would be tested often.

In 1920, a group calling itself the Children's Protective Association began agitating for the removal of Chinese students from public schools, arguing that they posed a moral threat to other students and hindered their learning. The Vancouver School Board favoured segregation, until all but four of Vancouver's principals, supported by teachers, dismissed the idea. The episode reflected attitudes in wider society.

Another deep recession hit Vancouver between 1919 and 1922, and there was a resurgence of public anger toward the Chinese, who once again were scapegoated over the shortage of jobs.

In 1921, veterans' organizations, unions, retail merchants and others in Vancouver re-activated the Asiatic Exclusion League to press for more restrictions and clamp down on immigration. The League went door to door canvassing for support, and by the following year claimed 40,000 members. This was something the federal government found hard to ignore. On July 1, 1923, the Chinese Benevolent Association's worst nightmare came true. Ottawa adopted a new Chinese Immigration Act, which finally followed the example set by the United States 41 years before and slammed the door shut on all Chinese immigration, with only the most extraordinary exceptions. Ironically, the measure was brought in on Dominion Day, the day Canadians were expected to celebrate their nationhood. The Chinese called it Humiliation Day and celebrated by going on strike. Many returned to China at the first opportunity and Canada's Chinese population went into a precipitous decline. Over the next 24 years, only 44 Chinese would get by immigration officials. By 1931 the proportion of ethnic Chinese in BC would drop to four percent, down from a high of 15 percent. In real numbers Asians in BC would decline from 35,000 in 1921 to 15,000 in 1951. The effects of the law for Tong's generation were significant. It meant he would grow up in a remnant population cut off from its old-world roots. Women and children would continue to be scarce and his world would be dominated ever more by aging bachelors, but "local-borns" like himself would come to occupy a larger place. The implications for Chinese businesses like Hok Yat's, which depended on Asians for their trade, was obvious and alarming. It meant that reaching beyond the Asian community would be essential if they were to achieve significant growth in the long term.

Hok Yat encountered another, more personal, setback in 1922. Admitting that he had been feeling poorly for some time, he made a rare visit to a Western doctor and learned that he had become a diabetic. Although the Canadian physician Dr. Frederick Banting had discovered insulin in 1921 and diabetes was no longer the death sentence it had been, Hok Yat doesn't seem to have subscribed to the new treatment. He followed a special diet of meat, vegetables and a kind of whole wheat muffin, in which he apparently placed great faith. It was Tim's job every Friday after school to go down to a French bakery on Robson and get a week's supply. Hok Yat's condition progressed slowly, but it was a serious one that forced him to admit to some new limitations.

Tong's elementary school years were uneventful. He described himself as an average student who pulled in decent but not outstanding marks. He took his father's advice and did his best to avoid trouble, although he asserted himself when he had to. John Lowe, who first met him when he was nine and Tong was 14, said he was "scared of him" because Tong projected the feeling that he would take no nonsense.

Another school friend, Fred Chu, who was in grade eight with Tong at Strathcona, remembers his thoughtfulness. There were four other Chinese in the class, each a good student, eager to get somewhere in life, and determined to make a good impression in the community. When Miss Bessie Johnston, their homeroom teacher, became ill, Tong came up with the idea of taking up a collection and buying her a bouquet of flowers—a gesture that both surprised and touched her.

Once elementary school was behind him, Tong went to Britannia High, having easily passed the mandatory matriculation exams that blocked the way for so many immigrant children. High school opened new horizons for him. The discipline of elementary school was replaced by a less restricted routine where

and collecting payments from the restaurants, grocery stores and laundries in the immediate area.

The city had emerged from a post-war readjustment and unemployment period. The port was becoming busy again as the implications of the Panama Canal took effect. Originally Vancouver was only seen as a shipping point to Pacific destinations. It took some time for the rest of Canada to realize it was also an ice-free alternative for shipping to Atlantic destinations, unlike Montreal. The federal government built a grain terminal in 1916 but it sat dormant for six years. Now grain trains were arriving around the clock to deposit Prairie wheat, and new elevators were rising like medieval towers on each side of Burrard Inlet. Radios were just coming into common use, and two radio stations had established themselves in Vancouver. Electrical appliances were wooing housewives but Hok Yat resisted these temptations. His business was improving but he reinvested most of his profit to increase inventory and improve service. In 1925 he bought his first delivery truck, a Model T Ford. It proved such a boon he exchanged it in 1928 for a much larger Chevrolet two-ton. In 1929 he bought the empty lot next door at 254 East Georgia and built a one-storey brick building with four bedrooms and a good-sized living room. At last Young Shee had a decent kitchen and modern washing facilities.

Hok Yat's reputation for reliability, honesty and willingness to provide service was winning ever-increasing support from his customers, but he was still meeting resistance in obtaining the quantity and quality of product he needed from the major suppliers. Tong was beginning to get a feeling for the business as well. His energy, outgoing personality and basic business skills attracted the notice of everyone who came through the door.

Girls also noticed him. Emeline Chong remembers him at the age of 17 as a "big, friendly boy," while

BY THE TIME HE WAS 17, TONG'S GOOD LOOKS AND EASYGOING MANNER WERE ATTRACTING ATTENTION FROM THE OPPOSITE SEX. "ALL THE GIRLS CHASED HIM," SAID FRIEND MARY YIP.

students could begin to exercise more initiative, studies took on a more contemporary significance and the sports programs were structured and well coached. Tong thrived in this new environment, even though he now had even more responsibilities working for the family business—sweeping the floors, helping to unload freight and stock shelves, making local deliveries,

another childhood friend, Mary Yip, states that "all the girls chased him." Occasionally he would see Geraldine Seto when she dropped in from her home in the remote West End to attend social events and youth activities. There were four years between them but her poise and maturity caught his attention. She had the rare distinction of being a third-generation British Columbian and it gave her a sense of ease moving between Canadian and Chinese ways that Tong admired. They became friends.

Tong wasn't entirely immune to the attention directed his way by the older girls. John Lowe recalls sessions where he, Tong and Tim, tried to teach themselves to dance, using brooms as partners. The results weren't impressive. Lowe's wife described the boys' dance style as: "One-two-three-four slow; and one-two-three-four fast."

When Tong and his pals wanted to do guy stuff, they went out onto a playing field or headed over to "Wingo's," a little drugstore run by Wing Y. Wong at

ED LOUIE (CENTRE) WITH A YOUNG H.Y. LOUIE DRIVER AND GUM HO LOUIE, A VISITING FAMILY MEMBER FROM THE CHINESE VILLAGE OF DOO TOW.

the corner of Pender and Gore. Wingo, who was considerably older than Tong and his friends, recognized the boys' need for a hideout and let them use his back room to play poker and "500" for penny stakes. It was about as far down the path of dissolution as Tong dared go. His father was as strongly opposed to gambling as he was to alcohol and drugs.

Tong kept up his studies at high school, getting decent marks while still finding time for a variety of sports, including soccer, basketball, rugby, and track and field. He played for several years on the Chinese Students Football Club team. Every member of the team was born in Canada and they more than held their own with other teams in the league. In 1933, they were the BC mainland champions and, in other years, collected the Iroquois, Spalding, and Wednesday League trophies, capped by the Mayor L.D. Taylor trophy for "the most sporting team both on and off the field in the City of Vancouver." Whenever and wherever they played, the crowds gathered. In its own way the team raised the image of the Chinese community.

Improving the community image was something Chinatown kept trying to do. Earlier generations of immigrants, who still thought of China as their homeland and harboured thoughts of returning, may not have cared so much, but to this new generation of young people born in BC, proving their worth as Canadians was more important than ever. As Helen Wong, a long-time friend of Tong's, explained, "Chinese youth, in the period between the two wars, was a splendid generation, well educated, well brought-up, but still handicapped by racism."

Against formidable odds, many of them would emerge in later years with established professions and businesses. Tong made life-long friends at this point, although some of them, like Fred Chu and Victor Won Cumyow, he wouldn't see until they met again years later.

CHINATOWN'S PENDER STREET IN 1929.

Photo: Stuart Thomson

W.H. MALKIN, ONE OF HOK YAT'S MAIN COMPETITORS, MOVED TO RESTRICT CHINESE MERCHANTS WHEN HE BECAME THE MAYOR OF VANCOUVER IN 1929.

Tong's schooling came to a sudden halt in his second year of high school when he contracted a severe kidney infection that laid him low for a year. The experience depressed him—he was held back in school and couldn't take part in sports. The year of his illness, Vancouver's Percy Williams broke the record for the 100- and 200-yard dashes at the Amsterdam Olympic Games. Tong was a track and field enthusiast and while Williams' remarkable achievement excited him, it also brought him face to face with the fact he was so ill he couldn't even walk, let alone run. Ultimately, he returned to high school and graduated in 1930 with good marks. His father's business continued to improve but still ran into difficulties, many of them caused by the ongoing discrimination. In 1927, the provincial government passed laws regulating how much produce was allowed onto the market and at what price it could be sold for.

It was a measure ostensibly aimed at stabilizing the incomes of white farmers, but it had a devastating effect on Chinese farmers and wholesalers, whose freedom to follow their own rules was their only way of overcoming the disadvantages of their situation. Wholesalers like Hok Yat, as well as Chinese farmers, storekeepers and peddlers, saw the new regulations as a move to limit business activity. They protested the action by pointing out that the laws not only reduced the producers' returns but also translated into higher prices for consumers; the Chinese consul was dispatched to meet with government officials and farmers threatened to challenge the law in England. The most effective action they took, however, was to simply ignore the new regulations.

The next blow came in 1928, when a group of 143 Vancouver businessmen petitioned the provincial government to grant cities the power to limit the number of stores owned by non-whites. It was clearly an action against the Chinese greengrocers who offered their customers lower prices, longer hours and fresher produce than most of their competitors. The petitioners got what they wanted: a Trade Licenses Board Act soon went into effect, allowing municipal trade licensing boards to decide whether certain businesses would go "against the public interest."

Then, in 1929, one of Hok Yat's main suppliers, William Malkin, of the wholesale operation W.H. Malkin & Co., ran for mayor. Malkin had only ever given H.Y. Louie product grudgingly, and his election platform included a promise to end the expansion of Chinese businesses into Vancouver. In his opinion, their spread "constituted a menace and should be stopped by confining all Oriental stores to fixed Oriental districts." Malkin won, and soon after introduced the bylaw he had proposed to council. Other councillors rejected it, but it revealed the attitude of one of Hok Yat's powerful competitors.

CHAPTER 4

The Sesame Seed Affair

Tong could hardly have graduated from high school and begun his career in business at a worse time. The stock market crash of October 1929 hit Vancouver hard, replacing a long period of boom with an economic depression that would continue with unprecedented severity for 10 years. New building construction ceased, bringing the coastal forest industry to a halt. A world that couldn't afford to buy bread could hardly afford the luxury of canned BC salmon, and the canneries turned their workers out onto the streets to keep company with the displaced loggers. Grain shipments dropped by 1.75 million bushels in one year. Nationally, exports plummeted from $1.3 billion in 1928 to $0.5 billion in 1932. Unemployment soared to over 30 percent. Vancouver became a magnet for the hungry and homeless of the nation, and every train from the east brought hundreds of jobless men who hoped the mild coastal climate would at least keep them from freezing to death. By the fall of 1930 Vancouver had 7,000 men on relief and one bread line outside the First United Church on Hastings Street numbered 1,252 people. A shanty-town of packing-crate shelters stretched from Main Street down the shores of False Creek behind Chinatown.

As in previous hard times, Canadian Chinese felt the impact first and hardest. Cannery work, still a mainstay of the community's labour pool, dwindled to a fraction of normal levels. Discrimination became more virulent as competition for scarce means of survival intensified. Even the wretched shacktown on the borders of Chinatown was racially segregated.

Hok Yat had reason once again to be grateful that he held the means of earning his family's living in his own hands. Grateful, too, that he had chosen to make his living in the food distribution business. People could eat less, but they couldn't stop, no matter how bad things got. He had to work harder and longer and take fewer risks, but he had been at it long enough now that he was able to keep the business on its feet.

On the other side of the ledger was a development that must have given Hok Yat great satisfaction. His sons were joining him in the business, more than making up for his declining strength by making it a true family enterprise. It was the dream of many a father in

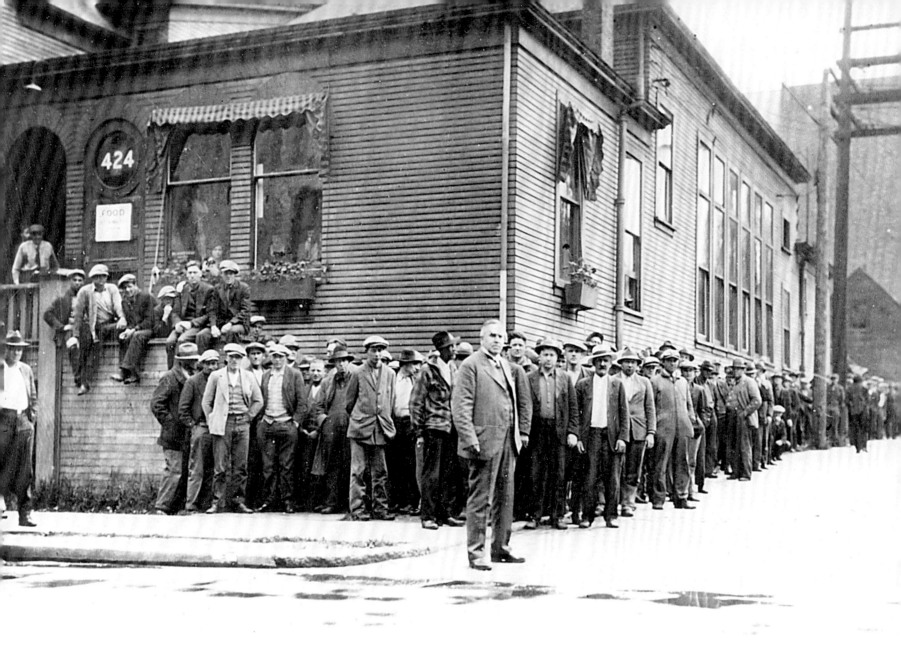

business for himself, and it had come true for him. What was more, the boys were up to the task. Everybody could see that Tim was a fine young man—handsome, strong, intelligent, responsible. A son to be proud of. And Tong the same, except maybe with a little bit of the typical younger brother's easygoing and daring nature, a little more pepper. That was all right. There was room for some spark and risk-taking in the secondary position, with the steady hand of the elder brother at the helm. Bill was a fine specimen, too. They all were. Against all odds Hok Yat and Young

Shee had performed the miracle. The greatest boon a patriarch could hope for was his: worthy heirs. Together they would overcome all obstacles and create a family dynasty in this new country. This was Hok Yat's vision, shining brightly from the depths of the Great Depression.

Tim had already begun working full-time when Tong finished school and Bill would be following close behind. As usual Hok Yat shielded his inner feelings under a stern exterior, subjecting the new recruits to a demanding training process. Perhaps it was with

A DEPRESSION-ERA
DEMONSTRATION WEAVES ITS
WAY PAST THE TROCADERO CAFE,
ONE OF THE GASTOWN BUSINESSES
THAT TONG CALLED UPON DURING
HIS APPRENTICESHIP.

thoughts of creating a more formal framework for the new generation to work within that Hok Yat took the step of incorporating his wholesale business in 1927. He had flirted briefly with the rather odd name "Louied's Company" but, when it came time to fill out the papers, happily opted for "H.Y. Louie Co. Limited."

With Tong now in harness, Hok Yat decided to invest in some additional education for his number one heir. He chose a college in Hong Kong where Tim could learn more about Chinese culture and language. He understood the greatness of his own culture and the slumbering greatness of China itself. Always gazing into the future, Hok Yat thought he could discern a time when oriental and occidental trading methods might meet on common ground, and a Pacific Rim economy would present great opportunities. He wanted his dynasty to be ready for that.

The cost of Tim's education strained their Depression-weakened resources, but it was manageable: $82.50 for passage in steerage, a small outlay for tuition and for Spartan food and accommodation. Tim

completed almost three years on this basis while Tong took over his responsibilities on the home front.

Tong's apprenticeship included everything from sweeping the floors and sidewalks to loading the shelves with stock, and keeping the inventory in order. He became familiar with the diversified product list and met many of the customers when they came calling to place orders or to discuss business with his father. In due course he was sent out to service some of the nearby restaurants, stores and laundries. Fifty years later he still remembered them vividly—the Peter Pan Cafe, Atlantic Cafe, Kings Cafe, the Trocadero, the Palace, Only Seafoods, the Homer Grocery on Homer Street, the Capital Grocery on Davie Street and many others.

Approaching an account for the first time, he never knew what his reception would be. The owner of the Golden Gate Cafe was one he could never forget.

"I had worked out a system," he recalled. "When I arrived at a restaurant, I went in the front door, sizing up sugar containers, catsup bottles, paper napkins, toothpicks, and that sort of thing as I passed the tables on the way to the kitchen. It gave me a clue as to what might be needed. By the time I reached the kitchen I could make a few suggestions to the owner or the manager. Mr. Thodos, the owner of the Golden Gate Cafe, read me the riot act when I came in the front door. He didn't want Chinese parading through his restaurant. If I was going to do business with him I should come in the alley entrance, and that was that. My pride was hurt but business was business. From then on I used the alley entrance."

In the Depression every customer was precious, and with the Chinese customer base shrinking, reaching out to people like Mr. Thodos was essential to the company's survival.

Ernest Krieger, a retired executive of rival food wholesalers Oppenheimer Bros. & Co., and a close friend of Tong's, was quite frank in this description of food distributors' attitudes in the days of Hok Yat Louie: "H.Y. Louie was regarded as an intruder," he stated. "Food distribution was then dominated by three major companies: Malkins; Kelly Douglas; and

Thompson Elliott & Company. They exercised their power to deny Louie the ability to purchase directly from major suppliers and thus place him at a cost disadvantage."

Charles E. Trimble, retired president of Oppenheimer Bros., seconded this statement. "The Chinese were not well thought of," he said. "In addition, the major distributors of that time did everything possible to block the growth and development of H.Y. Louie by threatening any and all grocery products manufacturers that if they supplied H.Y. Louie they would lose their business with them." All through this the Louies kept their composure and continued to work their plan even though they were forced to buy many items from their competitors at prices that left no profit for them.

At the same time, the Depression played havoc with H.Y. Louie's customer base in the Chinese community. Chinese workers had begun to be pushed out of the labour market in 1926 and 1928 when minimum wage laws were introduced first to the sawmill industry and then to the restaurant trade. This was beneficial for underpaid white workers, but as usual nobody was looking out for the Chinese. They had always received much lower wages than whites. They didn't like it, but racism put them at a disadvantage, and accepting lower wages was their only way of overcoming it. When the new laws forced employers to pay them the same as whites they were summarily fired. At one point in the Depression, 80 percent of Chinatown residents were jobless, leaving them with nothing to spend in the restaurants and stores that were the Louies' direct customers.

At least Hok Yat could provide food and shelter for his growing family. Others in Chinatown were not so fortunate. As many as 60 Chinese would pool their shelter money in order to rent and share a single room. Gambling halls with few patrons to cater to made their facilities available as shelter for the unemployed

DURING THE DEPRESSION, UP TO 80 PERCENT OF CHINATOWN'S RESIDENTS WERE UNEMPLOYED. MEN PASSED THE TIME BY READING NEWS POSTED ON THE SIDE OF A BUILDING ON PENDER STREET.

Photo: James Crookall

stiffened the backbones of many east-enders driven to the ropes by the blows of the Depression. A Vancouver citizen had risen from the skids to the heights.

Tong continued to perform his duties under the critical eye of his father, showing enough enthusiasm and energy to attract the attention of the customers and sales representatives. Among these was an ambitious young salesman for Vancouver Milling and Grain, who called on Hok Yat regularly to solicit orders for agricultural supplies. Arthur Laing was a statesman in the making, a latent political force with a fierce concern for the underdog and the victims of discrimination. He was impressed with young Tong's forthright manner and his willingness to take the initiative.

An example of this was the incident Tong referred to as "the sesame seed affair." In the early thirties, Hok Yat experimented with a new product, arranging to import 10 200-pound bags of sesame seeds from China. He soon discovered that the demand for sesame seeds was zero. The Chinese population regarded the seeds as a luxury product they could not afford at a time when the price of basic foods was often beyond their reach.

Two thousand pounds of sesame seeds were going begging until Tong decided to take a chance. He called on the purchasing manager of Four X Bakeries, one of Vancouver's larger bakeries, showed him samples of the seeds and suggested they might be useful in the baking process... as they had been in Chinese baking for centuries. The purchasing agent was non-committal. He accepted the package of sesame seeds and showed Tong the door. A few days later he reached Tong on the telephone to place an order for seven bags of sesame seeds. Soon after Four X Bakeries was introducing a new product: breads and rolls sprinkled with sesame seeds. It was successful with the public and quickly emulated by other bakeries. Hok Yat began to import and sell sesame seeds in considerable volume. He had taken note of Tong's imagination and initiative.

Chinese, who then became vulnerable to police raids. The Chinese Benevolent Society and other organizations set up soup kitchens and provided shelter in the Chinatown areas, aided and abetted by the Reverend Andrew Roddan, whose First United Church on East Hastings organized the largest soup kitchen in the city. The pugnacious minister had no time for racial discrimination.

Among the few causes for celebration in east end Vancouver was the victory of the neighbourhood boxer, Jimmy McLarnin, who won his first world welterweight title by knocking out the reigning champion, Young Corbett III, in 1933. McLarnin had attended Strathcona Elementary School, earning the devotion of every alumnus, including Tong. McLarnin, through his graphic display of tenacity, toughness and skill,

Arthur Laing saw these same qualities and became possessed of the idea they should be given the chance for further development at a university. He was himself one of the first graduates of the University of British Columbia's Agriculture Department, and he was high on the advantages of it. He discussed it with Tong, and Tong eagerly embraced the notion, but it was not a decision he could take; it was his father's call and there was little chance of his approval, with Tim overseas and a business to run.

Hok Yat was following the traditional Chinese way, grooming the eldest of his Canadian-born sons to take over the business in due course. His other sons would serve in lesser roles, with the option to start new lives elsewhere if that was their choice. When Arthur Laing presumed to suggest a university education for Tong, Hok Yat was dubious. Because it wasn't in his plans, he procrastinated, turning the thought over in his mind for some time. In his discussions with Tong, he suggested that any additional knowledge he needed could be garnered from the public library. Tong didn't really expect to get his approval, applying himself assiduously to his growing responsibilities as a salesman and general factotum.

His older brother returned from Chinese university in 1933, resuming his duties in the business and taking some of the pressure off Tong. His father then resurrected the matter of Tong's education. Perhaps Arthur Laing was right; perhaps he should not stop at providing higher education for Tim only. Tong also had intellectual potential that, once developed, would be an asset to the family. To deal with this complicated new age would take knowledge of the formal kind and the more you had in your corner, the stronger your position.

This time he would not go to the trouble of seeking a Chinese college. The University of British Columbia had opened a new campus on Point Grey in 1925 and with Depression attendance down to 1,600, it was crying for new students. The tuition fee of $125 a year could be managed; Tong would be at home, no extra expense there. And he would continue to work in the business after hours and on weekends.

Tong knew that few Chinese students ventured onto the developing campus of the University of British Columbia. In 1931 there were 27 Chinese students in the entire university, 10 of whom were women. After all, what was the purpose of a university degree when you were barred from the professions for which you trained? At the time Chinese were barred from entering law, the pharmaceutical industry, medicine, teaching in public schools, and working for the government. Arthur Laing's proposal that Tong should follow him into agriculture had the advantage that he was less likely to encounter a colour bar in that field, and in any case it tied in with the business in which they were both already engaged. Hok Yat bestowed his approval and, in the fall of 1933, Tong climbed onto a streetcar and made the long journey out to the University of British Columbia campus to register as a freshman.

Laing tried to brief Tong about what to expect on the campus. Since his childhood visits to the library and museum, Tong had idealized cultural institutions as places of refuge from the mean streets of the everyday world where minds might meet without prejudice, and he was looking forward to the university experience. Of course, it soon became clear that campus life was not so rarefied as all that. As a young person who had grown up within the strict confines of Chinatown, confronting the occidental world full-on for the first time, Tong could not avoid a heavy jolt of cultural shock, but he resolved to put a brave face on it.

Dr. Paul Trussell, much later to become head of the BC Research Council, was a student in the same year and department as Tong, remembering him as possessing considerable drive and energy. "He had a warm, outgoing personality," he recalled. "And a good

sense of humour." Trussell met him for the first time in the agricultural building common room where the 75-member class was assembled for briefing. "It was definitely a white, Anglo-Saxon male group for the most part," he stated. "There were two girls in our year: Joan McTaggart-Cowan, and Anna Rogozinsky, who was our class president." Tong managed to fit himself into this academic mosaic with a minimum of stress, at least none that was apparent to his fellow students.

"I think most of us came to know that Tong was associated in some way with a little outfit called H.Y. Louie in dry grocery wholesale...something like that," Trussell remembers. "Tong was definitely more business-wise than the rest of us greenhorns. We didn't know where we were going in our lives, but he seemed to have a strong sense of direction."

Another of his classmates, Jack Campbell, remarked on Tong's love of sports and athletics. "I played basketball and he turned out for track and soccer," he said, "but the family business kept Tong from participating as much as he would have liked."

Tong recalled his university years with considerable fondness. "The results were different there," he said. "The common goal was to get an education, and that united us. The Depression had an effect too; we took life pretty seriously." He admired the no-nonsense approach of the faculty, in particular, Dr. David Laird, head of Agronomy and Soil Sciences. "He combined all the necessary theory with sound, practical advice," Tong said. "His attitude was that you couldn't cultivate a cabbage with a slide rule alone, and we got the message."

If Tong participated in any of the perennial undergraduate hijinks, he didn't admit to it. Paul Trussell believes Tong may have been present at an uninhibited Aggie pep meet in 1935 or 1936. "It was held in the auditorium building and we had the Cariboo Cowboys on stage for musical backup. One of

OPPOSITE: TONG WITH HIS YOUNGEST BROTHER KENNY.

ABOVE: LO GI WORKED IN THE H.Y. LOUIE WAREHOUSE FOR YEARS CAREFULLY SAVING HIS MONEY FOR HIS EVENTUAL RETURN TO CHINA.

WILLIS WATCHES OVER A NEW SHIPMENT OUTSIDE THE H.Y. LOUIE WAREHOUSE.

our classmates, Phil West, who had his wild moments, got on stage with someone's six-shooter and blasted a hole through one of the Cowboy musician's Stetsons. It brought the audience to attention in a hurry."

Tong pressed on with his studies, pulling down reasonable marks, and continuing to share company responsibilities with his father and brother. Others of the family were starting to prove useful and, while money remained desperately tight, Hok Yat could see the first signs of stability. He sensed that the company's

roots were taking hold, in spite of the ravages of the Depression. With his growing confidence he began to entertain new hopes for his children. If they were to truly be accepted on an equal footing in this adopted land they would have to elevate themselves above the status of mere hewers of wood and haulers of water. Seeing Tim and Tong succeed at university gave him better understanding of what education could do along those lines. He determined to find a way to give others of the family a higher education.

CHAPTER 5

Going Home

ith the business finally showing some stability and his sons relieving him at last of the sole burden for keeping the operation going, Hok Yat had time to consider something that he had been pushing aside for many years. This was his responsibility to his mother, now well into her nineties, long a widow and still residing in the little village of Doo Tow. He had seen to her welfare, sending money to her whenever he could afford to, and ensuring that his first wife and children gave her the care she required. But he had not seen her since his departure to seek a new life in Canada almost 40 years earlier. Her messages to him always included the wistful hope that she might see him once more before she died. In 1934 Hok Yat acknowledged that he had kept her waiting far too long and agreed to visit her. Who knows, maybe there was more to it than that. His health had been deteriorating and he may have sensed his time was running short, although he fully expected to return to Vancouver and carry on with business. In any event, he made all the necessary arrangements to leave the business in the care of Tim, Tong, Bill and two full-time employees and booked his passage to Hong Kong aboard the *Empress of Japan*.

Many Chinese immigrants decided to return to China during the Depression, reasoning that conditions couldn't be any worse in their homeland, and even if they were, it would be better to be destitute at home among family than abroad among foreigners

H.Y. Louie employees outside the warehouse in the 1920s.

who resented their presence. Unfortunately, things had not improved in China. The country had been in turmoil since the death of Sun Yat-sen in 1925 and was now nominally in the control of Sun's successor, the Kuomintang leader General Chiang Kai-shek, although he was carrying on an internal struggle with communist forces and an external one with the Japanese, who had occupied Manchuria in 1931. Banditry continued to flourish; a series of natural disasters had worked their toll on the people and the land, particularly in the south surrounding the Pearl River delta. Despite this chaotic situation, overseas Chinese flocked home, a trend encouraged by Canadian authorities, even to the extent of paying ship's passage for each and every Chinese passenger. All that was required was for each to sign an agreement never to return to Canada.

Hok Yat was careful to make clear he wished to pay his own way, intent only on performing his filial duty and then returning to Canada. Almost as an afterthought, he had decided to take Tong with him. Perhaps it was intended as a reward for his satisfactory performance at university and his obvious contribution to business. More likely it was the senior Louie's determination to instill in his son a deeper knowledge of his ancestral homeland, all part of his long-range plan.

In any event, Hok Yat embarked on his voyage back to Hong Kong and from there to his village, Doo Tow, where he was received with joy by his mother, now 92 years old. Two months later, having finished his second year at university, Tong packed his bag and took passage to Hong Kong, travelling third class on the *Empress of Asia*. It was his first trip of any consequence beyond the city of Vancouver and he would gladly have travelled steerage for the experience. Even in third class, he felt surrounded by luxury and was thrilled to be introduced to foods and services beyond anything he was accustomed to. Many years later, well able to afford first-class accommodation anywhere in the world, he would think back to that first trip and smile, realizing that those third-class services had been very modest indeed.

His father met him in Hong Kong and travelled with him back to the village where, by now, he had re-established his connections not only with his mother, wife and children, but with the villagers themselves. Tong's grandmother welcomed her grandson with great affection and he settled into a new and unaccustomed way of life.

The dwelling place was an unserviced cottage by Canadian standards. Tong and his father shared a small room on the upper floor, a situation that must have struck Tong as strange, since he had never been in close physical proximity to his father for an extended period of time. He was afraid they would both have difficulty keeping up a conversation. Hok Yat was not in the habit of sharing confidences or indulging in small talk with his sons and daughters, and they were even less in the habit of chatting with him.

TONG TOOK THE *EMPRESS OF ASIA* TO HONG KONG IN 1934. THE THIRD-CLASS ACCOMMODATION WAS MORE LUXURIOUS THAN ANYTHING HE HAD EXPERIENCED BEFORE.

Photo: James Crookall

HOK YAT HAD THIS PORTRAIT
TAKEN SHORTLY BEFORE HIS FIRST
AND ONLY RETURN VISIT TO CHINA
IN 1934.

Whether by plan or lucky accident, being thrust together had the best possible result. Hok Yat turned out to be in an uncharacteristically communicative mood and initiated many conversations. For the first time the son and father found themselves enjoying each other's company in a warm and caring way. Those weeks they shared together in his father's village made a deep impression that would mark Tong for the rest of his life.

Hok Yat opened up to his son, outlining the far-reaching plans he had for the family business and detailing the way in which it should be conducted. While he said nothing to undermine the traditional leadership role of the older brother, he seemed to want to make sure his second-in-command was fully apprised of his plans, just in case. Keen judge of character that he was, he might well have sensed the rare gifts that reposed in Tong, gifts capable of carrying the family enterprise to the heights its founder envisioned, and far beyond. Tong himself was never very explicit about what transpired between them, though he left no doubt of its profound effect on him. It's unlikely that Hok Yat's confidences extended much beyond the subject of business, since that was the subject upon which his entire life was centred, but there were times, in the course of wandering through the village or among the fields and rice paddies when the conversation became more casual. It was one of those insightful moments when the child glimpses the parent not as an archetype, but as a flesh-and-blood mortal like himself. Tong could see how his father had lived in China, and how hard he'd had to work just to eke out a marginal existence. Life in Canada was undeniably better, marred principally by the many cruelties of discrimination. He could understand why his father had chosen to leave the village and take his chances in a foreign land and he could see why he had elected to make that foreign land his home. If he had never before fully appreciated his father's fierce dedication to making a secure life in Canada, he did now. Like a youth emerging from some powerful initiation rite, he took that fierce dedication upon himself.

ALTHOUGH HALF A WORLD AWAY, HOK YAT CONTINUED TO GUIDE HIS SONS THROUGH THE NUMEROUS LETTERS HE WROTE HOME FROM CHINA.

WHEN HOK YAT LOUIE TRAVELLED back to China his mind never strayed far from his family or his business back in Canada. While Tong benefitted from the lengthy conversations he had in Doo Tow with his normally austere father, some of Hok Yat's other sons regularly received letters containing instructions for, and inquiries about, the H.Y. Louie Co. Ltd. In these letters Hok Yat also outlined his personal philosophy and some of the principles he followed as a merchant—principles that gave him his reputation as a reliable and honest businessman. Long after his death, these principles would guide his sons in their business dealings and help them build the company into what it is today.

Below are two of the letters he sent to Bill Louie.

My Son Bill,

You must have learned through Tim and Tong the events and places I passed through since getting on the boat for Hong Kong. Now that I have a few spare moments, I will write you a few words of advice . . . Young people should always be earnest in your work. Treat your customers with trust and loyalty. Honour your mother; to your older brother, show respect. To your younger brothers and sisters, offer them good advice. That is what pursuit of happiness in life is about. When pursuing prosperity you must follow the laws of heaven. Don't be afraid to be kind and charitable. Ill deeds should be avoided. These are my words of advice for you to preserve and treasure and to remember.

Your father,
Hok Yat
March 30, 1934

My Son Bill,

I received your report on the progress of business and your progress in learning the basics of the business to the benefit of our family. We, as father and son, brother with brother, in the pursuit of a good living, [should plan] expenses and expenditures . . . as things progress. The execution of these plans is left to yourselves so long as you set your goals based on the business' profitability. It requires work and care not to step out of the focal point. Young people are always anxious, but their minds can be very simple. Under the present situation your older brother Tim is the manager of the business. His authority encompasses all cash coming in and going out, buying and selling, and all customer accounts. A manager's duties are heavy. It takes up a lot of time. As brothers you should cohesively work together and assist whenever you can. Discuss problems with each other. The older brother is a friend and the younger brother must show respect. Hope you will remember this so that the business will remain stable. For a learner . . . must be prepared to spend nights to study and memorize what is taught. You can concentrate on the bookkeeping work. Do it with a clear head. The more you learn, the better you get. One precious lesson to learn is that you do not have to rely on others. You learn to be sharp. Develop your own character as well as your working skills. Always remember to honour your parents, especially your mother who has the task of bringing you up. By following their wishes you are honouring them.

Your father,
Hok Yat
July 23, 1934

Deeply moving as it was for all concerned, Hok Yat's visit to the village of his youth was intended to be no more than that. He had come to say goodbye to his aging mother, and to pay his respects to his first wife and daughters. Having fulfilled his duties, he was anxious to return to Vancouver before business suffered from his absence. Tong had witnessed an astonishing transformation in his father, from the distant and secretive patriarch he had known all his life to a vulnerable fellow human full of hope, vision and caring. Tong was not the only one he reached out to. Further evidence of the turn his mind had taken at this auspicious time is to be found in letters sent home to his third son, Bill.

My Son Bill,

You may have got my note since my arrival in Hong Kong. After two months I have not heard from you. I am concerned.

It has been over a year since you had your studies at Ling Nam College. Now that you have spent time in a prestigious school, you should preserve your own reputation. Now that you are helping out in the business, you should assist in everything in the shop. Your older brother Tim is the manager and controls the business. You, as a younger brother, should help out in all matters and listen to his instructions as the manager. Be earnest, fair and loyal in your dealings with customers. Discuss things with your fellow workers. Be amiable to them. Show respect to your mother, so as not to forget her big task of bringing you up. Acquiesce to her wishes. When you have time write and let me know the affairs of the business and its progress.

Your father,
Hok Yat
May 27, 1934

It is as though floodgates had opened and Hok Yat couldn't wait to get home to communicate his thoughts to his growing family. His youngest, Ken, was only two years old. He sent Tong off full of advice and admonitions together with business instructions Tim was to carry out until his return. Then he went back to the cottage to spend a few more days with his mother, whose life, quite obviously, was coming to a close.

What passed unnoticed is that Hok Yat's own health had taken a sharp turn for the worse. He had been unable to keep up his special diabetic diet for months and the extreme tropical heat had placed additional strain on his weakened body.

Before Tong embarked for Hong Kong, he took a side trip to Shanghai, to renew acquaintances with his old school friend, Victor Won Cumyow. He discovered that Victor, his old Chinatown playmate was now going by the name of Vic Won and had become a Chinese celebrity of the first magnitude. "Elvis Presley couldn't have attracted more attention," Tong said. "He was an RCA recording star, attracting crowds wherever he went."

Tong took in one of Victor's performances at the Cathay Hotel where he endured the shock of being introduced by Vic to the entire audience. "Here I was, a stranger," he said, "a guy from a place called Vancouver being received by Vic like a long lost brother. Some of the prettiest girls in the place were begging me to arrange for an introduction to Vic."

It provided an upbeat finale for a memorable trip. Tong returned to Vancouver, feeling that many good and important things had happened. Within days of his arrival, word came that his father had died on November 23 in a Hong Kong hospital.

CHAPTER 6

Louisville Sluggers

*I*f Hok Yat Louie had experienced intimations of mortality, he mentioned it to no one. His uncharacteristic attempts to grow closer to his family in his final days, his sharing of confidences with Tong and his carefully considered letters to Bill, however, hint that he'd had premonitions.

The young man who had set out so hopefully from Doo Tow in the late 1890s and who had campaigned so determinedly to meet his obligations had come to rest back in his starting place at the too-early age of 59. Like the biblical Moses, he had laboured long and hard, laid down the law, seen a vision, but had never had the opportunity to experience the reality. But his vision would not die, for this son of the soil had planted his seeds well in the spacious land of his adoption.

Tim departed for Hong Kong with other members of the family, leaving the business in Tong and Bill's care while they attended the funeral. It was Tim's responsibility, as the oldest son, to represent the family and see to the proper internment of his father. In Tim's report he notes that Hok Yat Louie was buried outside the village of his birth, and "many of his old friends whom he had helped and befriended in Canada trudged many miles to pay their respects." Thirty years later, the family arranged to have his remains returned to Vancouver and laid to rest in Oceanview Cemetery.

Before the tragic news arrived from Hong Kong, the Louie sons had probably been counting the days until their father returned, eager to show him how well they'd carried on his work and anxious to ask a thousand unanticipated questions that had cropped up during his absence. And eager most of all to place the burdensome reins of the business in the more accustomed hands of its founder and master. Now they would never have those opportunities. Tim, the new 21-year-old head of the Louie family, found himself permanently saddled with the responsibility of looking after his father's widow and 10 younger children, carrying on with his responsibilities in the old world, and directing the family business. It must have been daunting beyond measure, as it must have been enormously comforting to look around and see Tong and Bill, his two sturdy brothers, standing in close tandem behind him.

Beyond the shock of their father's passing, it wasn't an easy time for them to get thrown into running the family business. Although by 1935 there were more restaurants in Chinatown than ever before, and 125 of Vancouver's 158 greengrocers were owned by Chinese, doing business wasn't easy. The number of Chinese-owned cafes located outside of Chinatown had decreased and the average Chinese person had even less money to spend than before.

At the beginning of the Depression unemployed Chinese men were given bed and meal tickets, qualifying them to eat and sleep in cafes and hotels approved by Vancouver's Relief Office. This didn't last long. Soon, jobless workers needed to become part of relief work camps, building roads in the province, in order to qualify for this kind of assistance. Because no separate accommodation had been built for them, and the idea that white people and Chinese people could share lodgings was unimaginable, the Chinese were excluded from the camps and instead given a third of the amount of assistance granted to whites. In explaining this decision, the city's relief officer said: "We can never expect Orientals to become self-supporting or even attempt to look for a job so long as they are getting more on relief than they ever earned in good times." At this time it was taken as a given that Chinese people could survive on much less than white people. This attitude extended to the soup kitchen on Pender Street, where the meals given to the Chinese were so meager compared to what was available at soup kitchens located in other areas of the city that 520 people signed a petition asking that it be abolished and that the Chinese be given the same amount of relief as whites. By 1935, it is believed that more than 100 Chinese men starved to death in Vancouver.

At the same time, white businessmen continued to take actions that worked against the Chinese. The year Hok Yat died, the BC Coast Vegetable Marketing Board was established in the Lower Mainland. Soon after the marketing board came in, bridges from outlying farmlands to the city were barricaded to prevent produce grown by Chinese farmers from reaching their wholesalers. H.Y. Louie supplied seed and fertilizer to the farmers in the spring, waiting for payment in the fall when harvests were sold. This new impediment to farm trade made it difficult, if not impossible, for H.Y. Louie to collect money.

The marketing boards were intended to stabilize farm income and did that in other parts of the food industry, but in market gardening they were a disaster because market gardening was traditionally a Chinese-dominated area and the marketing boards failed to represent the interests of Chinese farmers. This effect was not entirely coincidental. Editorials like this one published in the *Province* on March 2, 1937, make it clear new-wave Chinese businessmen like the Louies were being noticed and resented.

A decade ago Orientals were content to turn over their vegetable farm and small fruit products to the ordinary channels of trade in Vancouver and take whatever was the ruling price for that commodity. Today the situation has vitally changed. Production and marketing of all these household necessities is directed by smart young Orientals, born in Vancouver and claiming all the rights and privileges of Canadian citizenship. Twenty years ago lowly John Chinaman leased a parcel of land from its white owner and, mostly by hand, produced what he could peddle through the streets of the town. Today that picture is quite outmoded. Big Chinese corporations own large farms, equipped with up-to-date machinery, but still manned by the cheapest Oriental labor, working from dawn to dark; and their produce is sent to

OPPOSITE: HEADQUARTERS OF THE LEADING GROCERY WHOLESALER, KELLY DOUGLAS LTD., AT 375 WATER STREET. BIG WHOLESALERS LIKE KELLY DOUGLAS, MALKIN'S AND BC SUGAR DID NOT TAKE KINDLY TO H.Y. LOUIE'S FLEDGLING BUSINESS.

TONG'S GRADUATING CLASS IN AGRI-CULTURE, UNIVERSITY OF BRITISH COLUMBIA, 1938. BACK: PROFESSOR HOWELL HARRIS, UNKNOWN, GERALD BOWERING, DON KERR, NEIL HOCKIN, WILF PENDRAY, TED FENNEL, ROSS ROBINSON, PHIL BROCK, UNKNOWN, ALEX WOOD, DOC, HARVEY OZARD, PETER CRICKMAY. FRONT ROW: MAURICE WALSH, TONG LOUIE, DEAN CLEMEOT, JOAN MCTAGGART-COWAN, PAUL TRUSSELL, CECIL MORGAN.

market in trucks owned by Orientals, driven by Oriental chauffeurs, delivered to Oriental warehouses, sold finally through Oriental retail stores—where the salesgirl is very apt to be a brilliant young Chinese graduate of the University of BC. It is a changed situation indeed!

Chinese have crossed into the imported vegetable market as well. Wholesale Row of Water Street, supposed to contain some of the cleverest men engaged in the business, has had to make peace with the Chinese invaders. How long will it be before the latter are in command of the whole situation?

As the new president of H.Y. Louie, Tim managed the business much as his father had done, working tirelessly to serve and maintain his customers on the one hand, and to pay the suppliers on the other. In this period of forced transition, he and his brothers flew by the seat of their pants, trying to guess what their father's strategy would have been in the face of the money problems confronting them. Both Tim and Tong found it difficult to carry on the one-to-one relationships with suppliers and customers developed by Hok Yat over the years. He had based everything on trust built up slowly through many dealings and they felt themselves under close scrutiny as they went about trying to follow in his footsteps.

Nov 18/36

Sir:

Kindly excuse
Quan for being absent
from school last
Friday A.M. as he was
unavoidably detained

Tong Louie

PREVIOUS PAGE: OPPOSITE: YOUTH
WAS NO EXCUSE FOR GETTING OUT
OF WORK IN THE LOUIE HOUSE-
HOLD. WILLIS REMEMBERS TONG
MAKING HIM THESE OVERALLS
TO WEAR WHEN HE WENT OUT
"SWAMPING" ON THE DELIVERY
TRUCK AT THE AGE OF SIX.

ABOVE: A NOTE WRITTEN BY OLDER
BROTHER TONG ATTEMPTS TO
EXCUSE 15-YEAR-OLD QUAN FOR
MISSING A DAY OF SCHOOL.

They experienced increased pressure and obstruction from the big wholesalers who saw Hok Yat's death as an opportunity to bury the upstart company once and for all. Fortunately, most of the suppliers and customers Hok Yat had dealt with over the years remained loyal and supportive, including, of course, Arthur Laing. The company he worked for, Vancouver Milling and Grain, had now become Buckerfields and, as long as he was there, H.Y. Louie could count on getting a steady supply of agricultural products at fair prices. The many people in the Chinese community who had regarded Hok Yat as a friend and mentor also remained supportive. Posthumously, the Sunday meetings over which he had presided were paying dividends. However, while H.Y. Louie's reputation and credit was good with suppliers and tradesmen alike, it wasn't with the banks. When the company had a problem with cash flow, Tong went to the Royal Bank to ask for a $2,000 loan. The bank manager, Mr. McFadyn, spent little time with him and refused the request.

Tong did not return to university until the fall of 1935. With two years completed toward his agriculture degree, he wanted to finish, but it was hard to get the time away from business. He graduated from UBC in 1938 with a degree in agriculture, majoring in soil sciences. Following behind him on the campus was Quan, a younger brother he had encouraged to go to university, telling him it was a way to do better in life. Tong and Quan were particularly close, Tong serving as both role model and confidant for the younger brother.

Once he graduated, Tong was confronted by a major decision. Arthur Laing's advice that he would be able to find work in the agricultural field proved correct. Soon after he received his degree he was offered a job by Consolidated Mining and Smelting in Trail, BC. The giant company had a flourishing fertilizer division and was looking for qualified technical staff. They offered Tong a $90 a month salary, with the proviso that he move to Trail. Obviously this would give him a professional career, a princely income compared to what he was used to, and free him from the uncertainty and stress of the family business. The Depression was hanging on like grim death and the boys were being tested trying to protect H.Y. Louie from its competitors, but Tim was gaining his feet in the trade and with Bill and the younger boys backing him up, Tong could not honestly say that the company's survival depended on him. The Trail job would have been a dream come true for most young men of that time and it was, after all, what he had trained for. Nobody on earth would fault him for taking it. On the contrary, most would feel he would be passing up a great opportunity if he didn't take it. Consolidated Mining and Smelting wanted an immediate reply, placing Tong in a decision-making squeeze.

He really had no choice in the end. Tong could not forget those final days with his father in Doo Tow. In that special time together he felt he had somehow been deputized to carry on what Hok Yat had started. He had been given the vision his father had not had the opportunity to give anyone else. It was a vision of a family enterprise that not only survived and supported them, but went on to greater success.

Tong turned down the Cominco offer, never again to make direct use of his agricultural training.

Tim appointed his younger brother merchandise manager in charge of purchasing and sales, a position that covered a wide range of responsibilities. While Tong had always been aware of the obstructionist tactics of the large wholesale food competitors, he was now in the front lines. On the occasions when he could buy the products he wanted, it was often at a price that made it impossible to earn a profit when he moved the product to his retail customers. He learned the ropes the hard way. One mistake occurred soon after he was given his management position.

Tong was at the counter one day when a customer approached anxious to purchase a small bag of sugar for his personal use. H.Y. Louie was in the wholesale business exclusively and had no mandate to sell retail. Tong bent the rules, reasoning that this was an isolated case in which the customer was expressing a real need. Charging the retail price, he filled the order, gave the customer a receipt and sent him on his way, little knowing that he had been caught in a sting. The "customer" was a salesman for Rogers Sugar, the company controlling the manufacture and distribution of sugar not only in Vancouver but in most of western Canada.

Tong's little indiscretion resulted in a severe penalty for the company. Rogers Sugar cut off the sugar supply for an entire year, leaving H.Y. Louie

scrambling for another source. Tong found a local broker, Wells Whitcomb, and was put in touch with another supplier. Soon Tong had arranged for delivery of bagged sugar from a refinery in Jamaica and was congratulating himself for the way in which he had outflanked Rogers. After a number of weeks in transit the sugar shipment arrived, having passed through the Panama Canal. Tong took delivery of the shipment, consisting of 10,000 pounds of granulated sugar contained in 100-pound burlap bags, each as hard as rock. Passage through the Panama Canal, notorious for its high humidity, had turned the sugar to stone.

Tong's solution was to go to Harkley and Haywood, the sporting goods store, where for $1.75 he purchased a heavy baseball bat appropriately labelled "Louisville Slugger." Armed with this, he returned to the company's little warehouse where, for the next several months, he and other members of the Louie family slugged away at sugar sacks to break up their contents.

There would be other times when his flair for innovation and eagerness to beat the competition would get him into hot water. Take the Gold Dust Twins affair. Through the grapevine, Tong learned that he could purchase Gold Dust Twins laundry powder, reputed to perform miracles in the wash tub, at an extremely favourable price. The salesman at the other end was talking in carloads, so without hesitating, Tong ordered one.

"I had no idea how much a rail carload was," said Tong. "When the shipment rolled into Vancouver, I knew I was in trouble. It took two days to unload the stuff and three years to sell it. We had boxes of Gold Dust Twins powder stored everywhere: under the beds, in closets, under stairways. I think our profit margin on a box was three cents."

Some of his other merchandising ploys were more successful. In those days, there were few regulations governing food product quality. People in the grocery business were pretty much free to do whatever they could get away with.

"Everyone had ways to cut corners and squeeze out a profit," Tong said. "It wasn't considered unethical. I prefer to call it creative. For instance, we would supply perfectly good bulk catsup to the restaurants that they would then funnel into Heinz Ketchup bottles in order to give it a little class. We had no control over what the restaurants did. Each business had tricks of the trade."

At university Tong had been exposed to a few courses in food technology, and now he improved his knowledge of the subject, browsing library books and experimenting with products back at the warehouse. In due course he came up with some winners. His recipe for compound mustard became popular with restaurants and grocers alike. Eighty pounds of flour, thoroughly blended with 18 pounds of pure, ground mustard seed, packaged in convenient quantities, and sold at a price substantially lower than any comparable product, pleased his customers and earned H.Y. Louie a reasonable profit. Likewise a blend of 80 pounds of confectioner's sugar, 17 pounds of gelatin and a choice of fruit flavours yielded a product which might not have rivalled Jell-O but which sold for considerably less. Restaurants placed repeat orders for his vinegar concoction, deemed perfect for fish and chips and other uses. The formula was simple enough: one gallon of pure vinegar mixed with five gallons of water resulting in a liquid that was soon in popular demand, at an attractive price and a good profit. Tactics like these enabled H.Y. Louie to get around unco-operative local suppliers. Acceptable products at lower prices generated goodwill and attracted new customers. The Louie brothers were doing everything they could to keep their father's business from being trampled by the big players, and it was working.

From time to time Tong made decisions that kept him humble. When the Campbell Soup Company of

TONG'S EARLY OFFICE WAS CRAMPED AND CLUTTERED, BUT ASSOCIATES RECALL THAT THE YOUNG EXECUTIVE IN THE SWIVEL CHAIR WAS AS FOCUSSED AND TOUGH AS ANY CORPORATE BIGSHOT.

Camden, New Jersey, offered Tong an excellent deal on a bulk purchase of their line of soups, Tong accepted readily. To improve his margin further he chose to have the large order shipped by sea instead of by rail. Tong had forgotten what happened the last time he tried this. Once again the Panama Canal was his downfall. When the cases of soup arrived in Vancouver, the tops and bottoms of the cans, attacked by the tropical humidity of Panama, had developed an ugly patina of rust. Once again Tong, and any member of the family he could enlist, spent late night hours removing rust from hundreds of soup cans with steel wool.

"The cost of the steel wool probably wiped out our profit," said Tong, "but it was another good lesson for me and the entire family. Before you make a deal, study all the angles. Once you sign on the dotted line any hidden problem becomes your problem."

DURING THE DEPRESSION MAYOR GERRY McGEER BUILT WHAT STRUCK MANY AS AN EXTRAVAGANT NEW CITY HALL AT TWELFTH AND CAMBIE.

The Louies' old nemesis W.H. Malkin had been mayor of Vancouver at the outbreak of the Depression, but it was the wrong time for a wealthy businessman to appeal for popular support, and he was soon replaced by the doughty old war-horse, Louis D. Taylor, back for his eighth and final term. In 1933 the 77-year-old Taylor was trounced by the man who will always be remembered as the city's Depression mayor, Gerald Grattan "Gerry" McGeer. Known as "the man who flattened the Rockies" because of his role in fighting the CPR surcharge on freight shipped over the mountains, McGeer was an ebullient orator once accused of having "inflammation of the vowels." He seemed to feel he could make the Depression disappear just by pretending it didn't exist. Surrounded by desperation and want, he blithely announced plans to replace the old City Hall at the edge of Chinatown with an extravagant new edifice at Cambie and 12th. When he ran out of money to finish it, he completed the project by selling "baby bonds." In that same period he elected to read the Riot Act to thousands of hunger marchers, unleashing a storm of protest. "Mayor Gerry" next chose to celebrate Vancouver's 50th anniversary in 1936 with, among other things, a new fountain in the middle of Lost Lagoon at the entrance to Stanley Park. This great fountain, ablaze with shifting floodlights at night, has been a cause of much admiration in the decades since, but at the time it was hard for those squatting hungry and cold in Stanley Park to view it as anything short of an outrage.

In their tireless efforts to keep pace with the competition, the Louie brothers actively sought out new sales opportunities, or took on customers whose needs were being ignored by the established suppliers. H.Y. Louie rebottled kerosene for lamps used by the Jewish community in its rituals. Candles were also available at a good price. For the Italians they imported a variety of grapes used in wine making.

"Before long anyone who wanted to make wine was placing orders for our grapes," Tong said. "It made for good business, and it built our reputation. We weren't in the same league with the big wholesalers, but the name H.Y. Louie was becoming familiar in the marketplace."

Ernest Krieger, the retired Oppenheimer Bros. executive, remembers the first time he met Tong. "He was located in a little building on East Georgia Street," he said. "There wasn't sufficient space for offices. Tong worked at a desk placed directly under a flight of stairs. He had to stand up with care." Tom Farrell, who later became a president of Woodward's department stores, has a similar recollection: "When I first met him he was seated at some kind of desk, surrounded by cases of Pacific Milk. But appearances didn't faze him. He was all business. He wouldn't have behaved any differently behind a mahogany desk in a carpeted office."

In order to survive in the competitive wholesale industry there was no way H.Y. Louie could limit its clientele to the Greater Vancouver area. The big wholesalers had reached out to the major population centres of the province and H.Y. Louie could do no less. Tong invested $300 in a used Model A Ford and began regular sales trips into the province's hinterland, travelling through territory that took in the entire southern Interior. His sales junkets usually lasted two weeks, and occurred throughout the year in every kind of weather. The first trips were eye-openers for him, as he steered his Ford anxiously along the narrow Fraser Canyon Highway on logs poking out hundreds of feet above the river, crawled up the formidable incline of Jackass Mountain and bounced his way over the ruts of two-lane trails charitably referred to as secondary roads.

"Sales representatives for other companies could travel by train," said Tong, "but that was an expensive way to go and we hadn't reached that level of success. Generating business in the province was the same as it was in the city—calling for patience, hard work, and establishing a reputation for a good deal supported by good service. It took time but my dad had convinced all of us that time could be our friend if we used every minute of it in a constructive way."

There was no best season to travel. In the spring it was mud; in the summer the temperatures reached high into the thirties; the fall brought some respite, but winter could be impossible. It was essential to have at least one spare tire and a serviceable jack; a little knowledge of automobile repair could be a lifesaver. Tong had the spare tire and the jack, but he knew almost nothing about mechanics. "I just turned the key in the ignition and hoped the car would start," he said.

One winter escapade remained imprinted on his memory. January 1939 found him on the road heading from Osoyoos to Nelson, navigating through ice and snow in temperatures dipping down to minus 25 Celsius. By the time he approached the little community of Rock Creek, night had fallen, and it was at that moment that his radiator began to spurt steam. Shortly after, the engine began to labour, putting him into a bit of a panic; he wasn't dressed to spend the night in a stalled Model A at 25 below. Easing the car into the ruts on the side of the road, he climbed out and made his way toward a few lights shining up ahead, feeling the cold biting through his city coat and shoes.

It was about a kilometre to Rock Creek, where some kind of commercial accommodation might be found, but in the knifing wind he doubted he could make it that far. There was a small house beside the road with lights on so Tong took a chance and knocked on the door. It was opened by a middle-aged woman who quickly sized him up and ushered him into the warm kitchen. This was another encounter Tong never forgot. "They sat me down in front of a hot stove, poured me coffee, fed me a good meal and gave me a room to sleep in," he said. "Next morning they served me breakfast and helped me get the car started.

TONG SPORTS THE COLLEGIATE LOOK WITH FRIEND JOHN LOWE AND BROTHER ERNIE OUTSIDE THE VANCOUVER CPR TERMINAL IN 1937.

"In Vancouver, if a Chinese fellow had knocked on the door of a white person in the middle of the night, he'd have been sent on his way. Generally speaking I found the people in smaller communities to be friendly to one and all."

He called on people in every community of any size: every small and large store, restaurant and laundry worthy of the name, every farmers' co-operative. They were "cold calls," initial visits with owners and operators without prior introduction or forewarning. Tong, unmistakably Chinese, followed in the footsteps of white sales representatives from the large wholesalers in Vancouver, daring to compete with them for whatever business there was to be had. It was slow going at first. Often he found himself in that perplexing situation, familiar to salesmen with small firms, of having to sell to his customers and simultaneously collect for overdue accounts.

"I couldn't undersell the big companies," he explained. "Our profit margin was considerably less than theirs. What I had to do was sell myself from the minute I stepped through the door to the minute I left. If I managed to get some business, Tim and Bill backed it up with reliable service."

CHAPTER 7

Across the Threshold

In September 1939, while Tong was busy stumping the countryside, Canada declared war on Germany and joined the escalating conflict that would be known to history as the Second World War. One implication was that the sluggish economy that had dogged Canadians since 1929 was abruptly transformed into a wartime boom. Another was that 40,000 would die in overseas action.

Canadians volunteered by the thousands, but Chinese Canadians found the situation less simple. For one thing, Canada didn't seem to value their participation in the war. Restrictions made it difficult to join, and those who were admitted tended to be relegated to KP duty on the home front. Vancouver city council passed a motion in 1940 demanding assurances that the federal government would not give Chinese the vote even should they distinguish themselves on the battlefield. Following the First World War, 80 Japanese-Canadian veterans were given the franchise in recognition for their service and the councillors apparently wanted to make sure this mistake would not be repeated. Ottawa responded by excluding Chinese Canadians from the draft. This was

enough to discourage many who were already having doubts about laying down their lives for a country that denied them the vote federally, provincially and municipally, maintained a blanket immigration ban against them, barred them from entering professions, banned them from public swimming pools and generally deprived them of the most important rights of citizenship.

The Louies had more reason than most to take the hint and stay home. They were still struggling to get on their feet following their father's death, and the business on which their extended family so depended was still in a precarious position. In the boom economy they were finally going to get the chance they had so long been waiting for. One might have expected Tong especially to avoid involvement, knowing he was so dedicated to the family company he had given up a professional career for it just the previous year. One might have expected it, but one would have been wrong. The Louie men immediately volunteered for active service. Tim was ruled exempt as head of the family, although that didn't stop him from running bond drives. Tong tried to join up but was rejected because of bad eyesight, a chronic problem that plagued him for the rest of his life.

Ernie Louie, refusing to take no for an answer, pushed his way into the army, realizing his ambition to serve as a paratrooper. Quan, having completed his second year at the University of British Columbia with high marks, joined the Officers' Training Corps on campus, then applied for active duty in the Royal Canadian Air Force. Because of restrictions placed on Chinese Canadians, the recruiting officer at Western Air Command was willing to accept him for ground crew services only. Quan persisted, citing his demonstrated qualifications in the Officers' Training Corps, his excellent academic record and his reputation as a top athlete. Eventually he wore down the recruiters' resistance and was signed up for aircrew training.

He emerged from training as a pilot officer bombardier, embarking soon after for overseas training in Halifax bombers. Promoted to flying officer, he was posted to No. 6 Group, RCAF Bomber Command, 420 Squadron, known as the Snowy Owl Squadron.

The Louie family's response to the war was one of all-out support, untempered by any reservations. It was remarkable considering the circumstances. But the family never questioned its decision to rush to Canada's aid in its hour of need. It was the country their father had chosen, and they were children of its soil, even if Vancouver city council and others had not yet accepted the fact. Armed with the legacy of farsightedness practised by Hok Yat Louie, they kept the faith that deep down people were better than they sometimes seemed—"men's natures are the same" as Confucius said, and given time, basic human decency would out.

Meanwhile, in the early years of the war the company's revenues were soaring as the result of an expanding customer base and healthy consumer demand. Its growing prosperity could in no way compare with the gains enjoyed by the large, well-established wholesalers, but it was enough to place the company on solid

ALTHOUGH CHINESE WERE INITIALLY DISCOURAGED FROM ACTIVE SERVICE IN WORLD WAR II, ERNIE LOUIE TALKED HIS WAY INTO THE ARMY AND BECAME A PARATROOPER.

ground. Banks previously uninterested in doing business with the Chinese interloper now gave the Louies a good line of credit.

Tong was 26, a university graduate, well established in a growing business, a notably eligible young man. Many of his friends were starting families and were beginning to tease him about joining the ranks of the Chinatown bachelors, that aging corps of male workers consigned to solitary lives by the chronic lack of Chinese women. After tasting the freedom of the open road Tong sometimes found it difficult to return to the crowded confines of the family premises on East Georgia and would have liked to start his own home, but most of the girls he'd chummed around with in his teens had long since been snapped up, and he rarely met anyone who shared his interests. Then one day he heard Geraldine Seto was back in town.

Maysien Geraldine Seto had first caught Tong's eye when they were children attending the Chinese language school on Keefer Street. She'd grown up in a white neighbourhood in the exotic West End and it set her a little apart from the rest of the students, although her family didn't lack for roots in the Chinese community. Her grandfather, Seto Fan Gin, had sewn tents for miners in the days of the Cariboo gold rush and her uncle, Lee Mong Kow, was a founder of the Chinese Consolidated Benevolent Association in 1884.

Her father, Seto Ying-Shek (better known by his anglicized name, Seto More), was a truly remarkable man. As the Pacific passenger agent for the CPR Steamship Line and a self-taught scholar who at one time served as vice-president of the Royal Astronomical Society of Canada, he enjoyed a level of respect and acceptance by white society that was almost unparalleled at the time. His studies also extended to Chinese history and culture. He spoke many dialects, was skilled in Chinese calligraphy and was a fine watercolour painter whose works were widely collected. He was active in the Chinese community

QUAN'S APPLICATION TO JOIN
THE RCAF.

and headed a study group that in 1923 presented the government with a four-point proposal for improving conditions among Chinese residents.

Geraldine's mother, Franny Lew Seto, was also distinguished. Born in Olympia, Washington, she was the first United States-born Chinese-American to graduate from high school in that country—a

QUAN IN THE **RCAF** TRAINING
SCHOOL 1942/1943.

landmark in US race relations. Franny Lew Seto had a thoroughly Western outlook that melded with the classical Chinese orientation of her husband to create a stimulating dynamic in the Seto household. It gave Geraldine confidence in moving between the two worlds, which impressed Tong.

Geraldine was still in high school when Tong started university in 1933 and when she graduated in 1936, her father decided to send her off to Lingnam University in China, so Tong didn't see her for a number of years. Geraldine had to flee from China when the Japanese began to overrun the country. She and other students were evacuated aboard a British destroyer and transferred to a passenger ship at Hong Kong. She would never forget the sight of aerial attacks and later, flames rising above the distant skyline. She returned home and finished her degree in biological sciences at the University of British Columbia in 1940, intending to study medicine.

The precocious teenager whose confidence and style had caught Tong's eye years earlier now rated as quite a prize. Attractive, accomplished, heir to a distinguished name, she was a temptation to every matchmaker in the west. Helen Wong remembers her as "tall, slim and good looking, and very gracious in manners. She always spoke softly and was calm and collected. A perfect lady."

Tong was only a struggling grocery salesman but he did have a functioning Model A and he began courting her energetically between sales trips to the Interior. They hit it off. Mary Yip remembers that "All the girls chased Tong, but Geraldine was the right one for him." They were both university educated—unusual for young Chinese couples of their day—they had both travelled in China, they were both at ease in the white community and they shared a vision of a better life for Chinese Canadians. "Tong and Geraldine had a lot in common, as far as personality goes," said Ed Hellinger, a friend in their later years.

It is unlikely Tong had an inkling then of the degree to which he would become a cultural bridge-builder and the degree to which Geraldine would be the perfect partner in that activity, but their similarity of outlook must have been exciting for both of them from the start. He wasted no time proposing and she wasted no time accepting.

That was the first in a series of quietly radical acts that would make up their lives together. It was still the custom at that time for parents to arrange marriages in Chinese families, but they acted entirely as individuals. Fortunately both families approved the match. Young Shee was especially pleased, aware that Geraldine brought to the family qualities that she had been unable to. Her humble background had deprived her of education and she had enjoyed only limited exposure to arts and culture. Giving birth to 11 children and raising them responsibly while coping with Hok Yat's stern expectations had occupied every moment of her time. Geraldine brought an element of gentility to the family.

The Setos also accepted Tong. His family was not the wealthiest or most prestigious in Chinatown, but he had a good education, something that earned high marks in the Seto household. It was hard not to be won over by his friendly, outgoing personality and his athletic good looks, which complimented their daughter's qualities so well. And then there was the fact that this affable young grocery salesman with his battered old Model A had a glint of something very special about him, if you were discerning enough to notice it, and Geraldine's parents were discerning people.

They were married in style. The wedding took place on April 9, 1941, in Saint John's United Church, with a reception following in the Georgia Hotel. It was a grand event attended by the many friends and relatives of both families. The anticlimax was that there was no honeymoon. Tong had business to attend to, and then there was the precarious matter of

THE CHINESE TENNIS CLUB OF VANCOUVER WAS A POPULAR PLACE FOR YOUNG CHINESE TO SOCIALIZE. IN THIS 1939 PHOTO TONG IS SEEN SQUATTING AT THE LEFT END OF THE FRONT ROW, QUAN IS THIRD FROM THE LEFT IN THE BACK ROW AND ERNIE IS 13TH FROM THE LEFT IN THE MIDDLE ROW WITH JOHN LOWE BESIDE HIM ON HIS LEFT. MEMBERSHIP INCLUDED DAVID CHIU, EDDIE WONG, JACK CHIU, KENNY LEE, FRED SOON, ART LEE, CHU FUNG, WILBERT LIM, VICTOR LOUIE, HARRY CHIN, LOW CHU, JACK LIM, HOPE BUNN, MUN LUM, HOHN LEW, CHUNG LAW, STANLEY CHA, HENRY YIP, GAN CHANG, LEM PON, FRANK WONG, WING WONG, BENNY CHA, JACK WONG, BILL LIM, QUENE YIP, ROGER CHENG, DORIS KWONG,

PRISCILLA LIM, CHUCK LAW, MERTON MAH, EDDIE PON, DOUGLAS MAR, NORMAN YOUNG, SIDNEY WONG, NELLIE KO, JEAN LOWE, LENA BUNN, CHOW LOY, SOMAN LEUNG, GEORGE MAH, EMMA LIM, TOMMY LAI, LESLIE CHAN, MARY CHIU, MABEL MAR, KAI MAR, GEORGE LAM, IVAN WONG, CHARLES LOUIE, SHUPON WONG, KING CHAN, JOHN LIM, JACK CHAN, THELMA CHO, DORIS CHAN, WALE BUNN, EDDIE LAI, JAMES WONG, JOE LAI, JOE GEE, ROBERT CHANG, JANET WONG, ANNA LAM, ELSIE SOON, BUCK S. CHUNG, TEDDY CHANG, CHIN MUN, GERALD CHAN, KWONG CHANG, LESTER CHAN, FRED CHU, PAUL L. YUEN, HERBERT LEE, HENRY LEONG, VERA LEE.

CANADIAN LEGION
WAR SERVICES   Sept 7 1943.

Dear Wee -
Thank you for your very welcomed letter. Your grammar is much improved since the last time.

I hope you weren't trying to B.S. me with the picture you sent. I'm rather doubtful you could handle a fish that size. I think even Al would have had trouble.

Regarding fighter aircraft

The Spit is far superior to the Thunderbolt whether you believe it or not. The only advantage the Thunderbolt has over the Spit is the fact that it can dive faster. But this is of little use as diving is unimportant in dogfights. The B-Fortress however, is a very good aircraft. Although it does not carry the load of the British Heavy Bombers, it is faster and has more protection for its crew. I myself would like to be on a Fortress but its more

CANADIAN LEGION
WAR SERVICES   194

than likely I get on big Halifaxes.

My bombing scores have been very good. So far I have had 3 direct hits. My gunnery scores have been good too. Six percent of hits is considered good. my score to date is 23%.

Well, all for now and write again when you have time.

Quan

P.S. Don't forget to study hard this year.

IN A LETTER TO YOUNG WILLIS, FLYING OFFICER QUAN LOUIE KIDS HIS LITTLE BROTHER ABOUT HIS FISHING PROWESS AND TALKS ABOUT THE WARPLANES THAT ENTHRALLED YOUNGSTERS OF THE DAY, BUT ALSO PRAISES THE BOY'S GRAMMAR AND URGES HIM TO STUDY HARD.

moving into a new house. Tong often regretted that they hadn't elected to cap a perfect wedding with an idyllic honeymoon, but at the time he felt he couldn't do it. The company business made its demands, but even more pressing was the task of setting up house, an undertaking that was about to become their second, and much more radical, act of trail-blazing.

A few months before they were married Tong bought a house at 5810 Highbury Street in the exclusively white middle-class Dunbar–Southlands neighbourhood. By the end of the century it would be heavily settled by Chinese-Canadian families, and there may have been a few living above their stores or laundries at that time, but Tong and Geraldine were the first to attempt to occupy a regular home on an equal footing with their white neighbours. It was nothing new to Geraldine, since she had lived with her parents on this basis in the West End, but the reaction to her and Tong's plans showed just what an exception to the

rule the Setos had been. News of the Louies' planned move sent shock waves through the city.

According to the *Vancouver Daily Province*, in February 1941, a delegation of 23 residents, brandishing a petition with 83 signatures, arrived in front of city council. Tong's new neighbours urged council to take "instant steps ... against the intrusion of the Oriental into desirable residential districts," asked for lower tax assessments in the Highbury area because of "the occupancy of the Chinese" and appealed for restrictions "to prevent repetition of this occurance[sic]."

The protest became front-page news in the daily papers. Politicians were quick to exploit what they interpreted to be a major wave of public indignation, especially Alderman Halford Wilson, whose anti-Asian opinions were in no way softened by news that Vancouver's Chinese subscribed more per capita to the war effort than any other ethnic group in Canada. "This is only an indication of what will face the city

IN HIS MID-TWENTIES AT THE
OUTBREAK OF THE SECOND WORLD
WAR, TONG WAS AMBITIOUS,
EDUCATED, HANDSOME—IN ALL,
A NOTABLY ELIGIBLE BACHELOR.

years to come," he declared. "Where one Oriental buys property another follows." Wilson discounted previous rulings from the city's legal department that the city had no power to discriminate regarding races, arguing that Asians were already discriminated against in Vancouver insofar as they had no civic vote, were barred from the legal profession and their numbers were restricted in the fishing industry. He urged council to do what he incorrectly believed had been done in other cities like Toronto, and draft a bylaw that would prevent Asians from owning—or even renting—property in places other than "their own recognized localities." He was, however, willing to make an exception in order to accommodate white people who employed "Oriental house boys with rooms on the premises."

The newlyweds found themselves at the centre of a storm of controversy. While council soon discovered it lacked the power to legally ghettoize Asians and could only advise Point Grey residents to add

IN THE EARLY **1940s** DATING SCENE, FORMAL DANCES ARE THE IN THING. IN THE BACKGROUND **QUAN** BOWS TO A DANCE PARTNER.

CHINESE MEN—DENIED THE VOTE IN CANADA—DEMONSTRATE AGAINST FASCISM ABROAD AT THE BEGINNING OF THE SECOND WORLD WAR.

anti-Oriental clauses in the titles of new subdivisions (a strategy that was used until much later) the incident was by no means one-sided. Chunhow Pao, the Chinese Consul-General, lambasted Wilson's proposal as "prejudicial, discriminatory and a gross miscarriage of justice and a reflection on the national dignity of China." There was a growing element in the white community opposed to racism as well. The Co-operative Commonwealth Federation party was outspoken in its condemnation of racial discrimination, of which the Louie housing affair was a prime example. As Kay Anderson notes in *Vancouver's Chinatown*, as people became aware of what was going on in Europe during the Second World War "the confidence of scientists in racial typologies waned considerably, and eugenics fell, if it had not already, into scientific disrepute." In a letter to the editor, a J.E. Boyd wrote that the "proposal to confine Oriental citizens to certain areas of the city is just another example of how some Canadians regard our minorities as inferiors. Decent-minded Canadians will not permit 'pure Aryan' ideology to take root here. Events in Europe prove that Aryanism rapidly leads to pogroms and ghettos." In another letter to the editor, signed by "A Second Generation Chinese," Wilson was ridiculed for complaining that the Chinese lived in squalor on one hand and was opposed to them trying to improve their living conditions on the other. The writer also took a stab at the residents of Southlands, pointing out their hypocrisy:

> When Mr. Churchill tells you that the Nazi principles of intolerance must be destroyed, you cheer. When Mr. Roosevelt made his inaugural spech [sic] that freedom shall prevail for all peoples, you are also in accordance. A final comment on his worship's statement that, "If anything can be done to segregate (Orientals) in the same district, we are all for it." When people openly commend the policies of Herr Hitler and Herr Streicher, we Chinese are ready for your Ghettos and concentration camps.

The flame of indignation was further fanned by a growing awareness of the Chinese Canadian contribution to the war effort. Geraldine's father had many influential supporters who gave quiet but effective support. The vast network of friends Hok Yat had built up over the years made their opinions felt. The well-connected Arthur Laing was also outspoken in his support of his long-time friend.

Whether or not Tong and Geraldine were aware of just what a stir their solitary move to desegregate suburbia would produce is hard to say, but it is noteworthy that once the whirlwind descended upon them, they gave no sign of backing down. Perhaps the single most influential occurrence was the wholehearted endorsement of their next door neighbours at Highbury. Miss Amy Leigh joined with her father in welcoming Tong and Geraldine into the neighbourhood and resisted any and all pressure imposed by other residents. This simple but unyielding gesture of approval was immensely important to Tong and his bride. Gradually the protest subsided and the young couple settled into married life. They and the Leighs remained close friends from that time on.

CHAPTER 8

War, Peace and Passages

Despite the reports of horrific destruction that continued to pour in from overseas, the general atmosphere was determinedly positive, particularly in the last years of the war when the tide appeared to have turned in favour of the Allies. Strict rationing of butter, sugar, meat, tea, coffee, liquor and gasoline seemed a small enough price to pay in view of the sacrifices made by others. While blackouts had been imposed regularly in the early years of the war, they were employed later more as a drill than as a response to real danger. Sirens sounded and the lights went out throughout the city, but this was not often. Downtown Vancouver at night was a cheerful sight, particularly along the Granville Street entertainment strip where the brilliantly lit theatre facades competed with every colour of neon tubing coiled around restaurant and store fronts.

Shipyards employed over 20,000 workers, hundreds of them women. Munitions factories were established throughout the city and out on Sea Island, Boeing Airplane had a workforce of 5,000 turning out planes and parts for allied squadrons. Existing sawmills were running three shifts, their output augmented by the production of new sawmills and plywood plants. The influx of workers from the Prairies and eastern Canada swelled the population dramatically, bringing more than 170,000 new residents to the city in a 10-year period from 1941. The population explosion fueled the expansion of districts and municipalities, a major housing boom, the construction of bridges, roads and highways fanning out to Greater Vancouver, the Fraser Valley and the hinterland of the province. More children created a need for more primary and high schools. The burgeoning population, together with the return of wounded servicemen, called for the enlargement of existing hospitals and the construction of new ones.

It was a time of high energy generated by the demands of the war and the prosperity it created; but also a time tempered by a persistent wave of sadness renewed each day with the publication of the latest lists of dead and wounded.

To Tong's everlasting sorrow, Quan's name appeared on the list. In January 1945, he flew his final mission in which his Halifax, separated from the rest of the squadron by bad weather, arrived over the target late and alone, an easy mark for anti-aircraft fire and fighter planes. The plane went down in flames over Magdeburg and two crew members parachuted to safety, but after some time Quan was listed as presumed dead. He was 24. It was a terrible blow for the entire family and for Tong especially, who had been so close to his younger brother.

His brother Ernie was luckier. Specially trained for action in the eastern theatre, in the final months of the war he parachuted behind Japanese lines in Burma where he was assigned to enemy surveillance—an extremely dangerous mission from which he was fortunate to return.

In 1945, he was among the 400 Chinese serving in the armed forces who were granted the right to vote. Despite the opposition that had sprung up over the mere possibility of this occurring just a few years earlier, there was little controversy. For the first time in British Columbia's history, the Chinese were receiving favourable media coverage because of their generous

ON JANUARY 19, 1945, THE TELEGRAM DREADED BY EVERY SOLDIER'S MOTHER ARRIVES AT 255 EAST GEORGIA. QUAN IS MISSING IN ACTION.

CANADIAN PACIFIC
TELEGRAPHS
World Wide Communications

W.D. NEIL, General Manager of Communications Mont

4WAFO 33/32 GB 2 EXA REPORT DELIVERY

OTTAWA ONT JAN 19 1945 221A

MRS H Y LOUIE, 1034
255 EAST GEORGIA ST, VANCOUVER B.C.

M9209 REGRET TO ADVISE THAT YOUR SON FLYING OFFICER QUAN JEW

LOUIE J THREE EIGHT TWO FOUR TWO IS REPORTED

MISSING AFTER AIR OPERATIONS OVERSEAS JANUARY SEVENTEENTH STOP LETTER

FOLLOWS

RCAF CASUALTIES OFFICER

1202A.

Chinese Soccer Star Missing After Raid

FO. Quon Louie, Four Other B.C. Flyers Fail to Return From Night Mission

Nine Canadian planes were reported missing following the great raids over enemy Europe on the night of January 16-17, when 1200 R.A.F. and R.C.A.F. night bombers struck at a German industrial centre and enemy oil refineries.

Operations on that night account for five of the six B.C. names which appear in the R.C.A.F.'s 1124th casualty list today.

All are listed missing, but later word to his wife states that Flt.-Lt. W. F. Borrett is believed killed and Mrs. Alexander Morrison has since received word that her only son, Flt.-Sgt. J. M. MacDonald is a prisoner of war in Germany.

Also listed missing is FO. Quon Louie, Vancouver-born Chinese soccer star, who left his studies at U.B.C. to enlist and who has a brother overseas with the Canadian Army.

The sixth name is that of PO. D. F. McAllister of Vancouver, who is presumed dead. German information is that he is buried in Ede, Holland.

MISSING.

FO. Douglas James Bailey, son of Mr. and Mrs. Thomas Bailey, 1978 Forrester street, Victoria.

Reported missing on January 17, FO. Bailey, a former president of the B.C. Conference, Young People's Union, United Church, was born in Victoria where he was educated at Boys' Central and Victoria High schools. He joined the R.C.A.F. in February, 1943, after working for a time at the Victoria Machinery Depot, and graduated at Edmonton in January, 1944.

Flt.-Lieut. William Fleming Borrett, whose wife lives at 3123 West Second.

On Wednesday, Flt.-Lieut. Borrett's wife received word from Ottawa that International Red Cross, quoting German information, said he had lost his life and pending further particulars was to be considered as missing, believed killed. He was originally reported missing as of January 17.

Flt.-Lieut. Borrett, pilot in a Halifax, joined the R.C.A.F. in 1941. He was born in Winnipeg, attended high school in Burnaby, and was married at Winnipeg in 1942. His father, Roger Borrett, lives in East Kelowna and his mother in San Francisco. A half-brother, George Foster, was killed last July on active service with the U.S. Navy.

FO. Quan Jil Louie, son of Mrs. H. Y. Louie, 255 East Georgia.

The third B.C. man reported today as missing following air operations over Germany on the night of January 16-17 is FO. Quan Louie, referred to in a recent R.C.A.F. release as "one of the most popular members of the Snowy Owl Squadron, where he has earned the regard of his squadron mates through his matter-of-fact modesty."

Flying Officer Louis was born in Vancouver, and after graduating from Britannia High School entered U.B.C., where he played intermediate basketball and won his big block letter for soccer. He had completed two years towards his Bachelor of Commerce degree when he left his studies to join the R.C.A.F. in November, 1942.

He graduated with his commission as a bombardier in October, 1943, and went overseas early in 1944. He was approaching the ___ his tour ___

nent Chinese businessman and founder of the wholesale firm of H. Y. Louie Co. Ltd. Besides his mother, he has eight brothers, of whom Pte. Ernest Louie is now overseas with the army.

Flt.-Sgt. John Morrison MacDonald, son of Pte. and Mrs. Alexander MacDonald, 6017 Vine.

His mother has received word, through International Red Cross, quoting German sources, that Flight-Sergeant MacDonald, reported missing on January 17, is now a prisoner of war in Germany.

Flight-Sergeant MacDonald, 20, whose father is serving with the Veterans' Guard of Canada at Red Deer, Alta., was born in Scotland and came to Canada in 1927. He joined the R.C.A.F. in 1943 and went overseas as a wireless air gunner in January, 1944.

Prior to enlisting, he worked in an aircraft factory at Fort William, where he had lived and gone to school. His mother moved here since he went overseas, and his sister, Margaret, is also here.

Flt.-Lieut. Elvet Baxter McCutcheon, son of Mrs M. B. McCutcheon, 8550 Heather.

Flt.-Lieut. McCutcheon, fifth B.C. man on today's list to be reported missing on January 17, was born in Vancouver and attended Richmond High School. Further particulars appeared in The Vancouver Daily Province on January 22.

PRESUMED DEAD.

PO. Douglas Fraser McAllister, son of Mr. and Mrs. J. F. McAllister, 3737 West Thirty-eighth.

PO. McAllister, 21, was originally reported missing on June 17, 1944, when the Halifax bomber in which he was navigator was shot down. His parents were later informed through International Red Cross, quoting German information, that he was buried in the Communal Cemetery at Ede, Holland.

A member of the Goldfish Club after being rescued from the Channel, following his third trip over Leipzig, PO. McAllister was on his thirty-first operational flight when reported missing.

He was born in New Westminster and attended school there and also Lord Byng and King Edward High schools here. He joined the Air Force in March, 1942, and went overseas the same year.

Besides his parents, he leaves a sister, Erma Jean, at home, and two brothers Jack A. and William K., both at school.

FO. QUON L. LOUIE. . . . missing.

FLT.-LIEUT. W. F. BORRETT. . . . believed killed.

FLT.-SGT. J. M. MACDONALD . . . prisoner of war.

PO. D. F. McALLISTER. . . presumed dead.

---

contributions to the war effort, their service overseas and their artistic and scholastic achievements. At the same time, as the full scope of Nazi atrocities became public, the white pride movement plummeted in popularity, and those who publicly opposed Asians receiving the franchise became increasingly marginalized.

In 1947, after consistent lobbying, the provincial government agreed to amend the elections act and granted Chinese-Canadian citizens the vote. The right to vote in federal and municipal elections followed. With the franchise came the right of Chinese Canadians to enter professions previously barred to them. For the first time they could become dentists, lawyers, pharmacists, and chartered accountants. In 1947, the discriminatory federal legislation enacted in 1923 restricting Chinese immigration to a trickle, was also repealed, though it wouldn't be until 1967 that all discriminatory immigration restrictions were removed. It had taken the better part of 100 years but finally the doors had swung wide. Chinese Canadians

QUAN'S DISAPPEARANCE MADE HEADLINES IN THE LOCAL PRESS.

THIS PAGE: TOWARD THE END OF THE WAR, PARATROOPER ERNIE LOUIE DREW A DANGEROUS ASSIGNMENT: DROPPED BEHIND ENEMY LINES IN MALAYSIA, HE OVERSAW THE SURRENDER OF A GARRISON OF 500 JAPANESE SOLDIERS. THIS CONQUERING HERO IS SHOWN IN 1946 ON HIS RETURN TO VANCOUVER.

OPPOSITE: A VICTORY PARADE MARCHES THROUGH CHINATOWN IN 1945. ONLY A COUPLE OF CHINESE FLAGS ARE VISIBLE AMONG THE UNION JACKS.

population had led to some remarkable transitions. Whereas before, Chinatown had been regarded as a malodorous ghetto, studded with gambling dens and laced with dark and dangerous alleys, now it became an "in place."

The people of Chinatown hurried to cater to this surge in popularity. Old restaurants were refurbished and new restaurants appeared, decorated to satisfy the white clients' notion of what Chinese surroundings should be. Grocery stores and gift shops burgeoned. All of this illuminated by a maze of neon tubing that bathed Chinatown's Pender Street in a rainbow glow from one end to the other. Vancouver's tourist industry hastened to put Chinatown on the list of attractions a traveller must see and experience.

This trend could only help H.Y. Louie and the company continued to acquire new accounts and to expand business well into the post-war years. Employment remained high, buoyed by the confidence BC industry had gained during the war. Housing developments continued to flourish and commercial strips sprang up along Broadway, South Granville, Kingsway and East Hastings. The Park Royal shopping centre, the first of its kind in Canada, opened in West Vancouver, later to be emulated by Oakridge Shopping Mall, setting the style for many more to come. High-rise apartments began making inroads among the stately mansions of the West End. Vancouver's population continued to climb, triggering an increase in services, markets and restaurants. H.Y. Louie rode this wave of expanding activity.

Vancouver's Chinese population was still falling but with increased prosperity it became a more viable market. Taking into account Chinese businesses only, H.Y. Louie had potential access to 474 laundries, 2,639 restaurants, 845 retail stores, and 3,220 farmers and gardeners, many of these in the more accessible southern reaches of the province. H.Y. Louie had built up a dominant position in the Chinese sector, and Tong

entered onto a playing field which, if not entirely level, was open to the horizon.

The picture continued to improve into the late forties. In 1946, Vancouver celebrated its Diamond Jubilee and its continuing prosperity, presenting a pageant on the stage of what was described as "the world's largest outdoor theatre" erected in Stanley Park. Chinese citizens were included in the performance. The changing attitudes of Vancouver's white

ON MARCH 6, 1945, Tong and all other Vancouverites got a grim taste of the terrible destruction taking place overseas. *The Green Hill Park*, a WWII Liberty Ship built in Vancouver, exploded at CPR 'B' dock at the foot of Burrard Street while it was being loaded. The blast shattered thousands of windows in downtown Vancouver, hurled pieces of cargo as far away as Lumberman's Arch in Stanley Park and killed eight men—making it one of the most frightening waterfront disasters in Vancouver's history.

The burning freighter was towed away from the dock to Siwash Rock where it was left to burn on the beach for the next several days. While rumours circulated that the explosion was caused by an anonymous worker dropping a match while stealing a bottle of whiskey, an investigation never found the actual cause of the explosion and no one was blamed for it. A report of inquiry did find, however, that the vessel's dangerous cargo was being improperly stowed and this was a major contributing factor in the blast.

Amazingly, following the war the 9,679-tonne freighter was refitted, renamed the *Phaeax II* and sold.

had expanded beyond this with his sales incursions into the provincial interior. As well, he was making some progress in the white business sectors, not comparable with the performance of the large, established wholesalers, but encouraging.

Despite all this progress, "caution" remained a key word at H.Y. Louie. Most profits were channelled back into the business in order to consolidate and strengthen the company's position, a long-standing policy that Tim Louie maintained. As president of the company and head of the family he sought to minimize risks. Keenly aware of how much his father had struggled to build the business to a modest level of success, his tendency was to exercise patience and prudence.

Although Tong's first son Brandt had been born on July 5, 1943, and his second son Kurt a few years later on August 5, 1946, his familial responsibilities were much less than Tim's. Perhaps because of this, and because his nature was more inclined toward experimentation and innovation, he was eager to try new ideas. From time to time, he gave the family reason to doubt, as in the hardened sugar and rusty soup can debacles, but other ventures, like the sesame seed promotion, were to his credit.

Brothers Ernie and Bill were now working full-time in the business, having completed their university education. Tim, encouraged by Young Shee, saw to it that there would always be money for education, even when there might be little for other purposes. In a time when university education was still largely a preserve of upper-middle-class WASPs and the rate of attendance by minorities was virtually nonexistent, the academic achievements of Hok Yat and Young Shee's children were truly remarkable.

DESPITE THE TENSION AND PRIVATIONS OF WARTIME, H.Y. LOUIE CO. LIMITED TREATS EMPLOYEES TO A CHRISTMAS PARTY AT THE W.K. GARDENS.

dynamic support. Although her life had not been easy, her consolation, if she gave it any thought at all, was that life in Canada had been better than what she would have endured in the Chinese village of her birth. She had joined Hok Yat Louie in this new, hostile land, had helped him make a go of it, had seen one son die, and had lived to see grandchildren.

Her death brought her life into focus and the family mourned her passing. When her husband died he left his entire estate to her. She, in her will, divided her estate equally among her 11 offspring. Each received one share of the H.Y. Louie company, a division which in due course would take on considerable significance. She was buried in Oceanview Cemetery, and life resumed its course for those she left behind.

ABOVE: HOK YAT'S WIDOW YOUNG SHEE, DRESSED IN TYPICAL WARTIME FASHION, POSES WITH HER THIRD SON BILL.

ABOVE RIGHT: YOUNG SHEE IN THE 1940S.

In 1948, Young Shee suffered a massive stroke and died soon after. She was 56 years old. Her husband had lived to see the beginnings of success in the business he had struggled to launch. His wife lived long enough to see it firmly anchored, with her son, Tim, in careful control, and her other son, Tong, providing

CHAPTER 9

An Idea a Minute

Tong's sons were too young when Young Shee died to have extensive memories of her. Brandt remembers his father speaking of her affectionately, describing her as a strong and caring woman. By comparison, the impression he gave of Hok Yat was of an authority figure who commanded respect, worked hard, expected his children to do the same, and left the raising of his family to his wife. It seems his example rubbed off on Tong.

Even when the children were young, Tong's work kept him away from home, taking him out of town on sales trips two weeks each month and requiring long hours when he was in the city. He and Tim were the principal breadwinners not only for their own households, but for the entire Louie family as well.

In the summer of 1948, Vancouver and the Lower Mainland experienced a major catastrophe. The Fraser River, swollen by the swift thaw of deep winter snows in the mountains, created a flood that swamped communities and farmlands from New Westminster to Hope. The resulting state of emergency saw the evacuation of 16,000 people and total destruction or damage to 2,000 homes. Vancouver's road link to the rest of the province and country was cut off and Tong's trips to the Interior were curtailed for several weeks.

By this time, Tong's mode of transportation had improved. The used Model A Ford he had started with, at a cost of $300, had served its purpose and he managed to sell it for $275—a deal that gave him satisfaction even when he thought back on it later in life. His sales rounds had begun to pay well enough so that he was able to buy better vehicles. He had built up relationships with some substantial figures, like Kelowna's Pasquale "Cap" Capozzi, the Italian vintner who made BC wine an industry. There was also George Kaiway, owner of Liberty Grocers in Nelson, who was always willing to share the latest gossip and sports speculation when placing his orders. Along the entire route, Tong added to his customer list and to his roster of friends. In later years, Charles Trimble, the retired Oppenheimer Bros. president, would marvel at Tong's ability to attract and nurture friendships.

"He likes people," said Trimble, "and that leads to friendship. His loyalty to friends is well known."

Fred Chu first became friends with Tong in 1925 when they shared a grade eight homeroom class at

Strathcona School. The two had been close, but then Chu moved away and they didn't see each other again until the 1940s, when he returned from eastern Canada to set up a medical practice in Vancouver.

"Tong heard about my return and made sure that he was my first patient," said Chu. "He was healthy as a horse, but it was his way of saying 'hello' again. We have been close friends ever since." Like Chu, Tong's old university classmate Paul Trussell moved away and didn't return for several years. He arrived back in Vancouver in 1947 to work for the BC Research Council after a nine-year absence. "Tong contacted me as soon as I returned to the city," he said. "Obviously he

(didn't) forget people. He asked me if I would help him develop a candied ginger product."

Trussell set up an experimental production operation in the basement of a warehouse. Together with a colleague, Dr. Bill Pearson, he worked on drying methods for three months. The experiment wasn't very successful. "The operation was too Mickey Mouse," said Trussell. "Tong agreed that we should close shop but that episode renewed our friendship." Occasionally, Trussell and others from the BC Research Council met in the Louies' basement to play poker. Although Tong could now afford to gamble a little more seriously than when he played in the back of

DESPITE HIS HECTIC SCHEDULE AND FOCUS ON BUSINESS, TONG CULTIVATED AND TREASURED LONG-TERM FRIENDSHIPS. TWO FRIENDS HE MAINTAINED FROM HIS CHILDHOOD WERE FRED CHU (SECOND LEFT) AND JOHN LOWE (RIGHT).

Wingo Wong's shop, the stakes hadn't increased much—the pots rarely exceeded two dollars.

Clearly, Tong didn't allow the attitudes of the day to get in the way of his friendships or his business dealings. Cal McLeod first met Tong in 1935 when he worked for Standard Brands. Like Tong, McLeod spent his entire life working in the grocery business, and the two were still friends when McLeod retired and opened the Grocery Hall of Fame in Richmond.

"Over the years I saw his business grow and develop. He worked like a beaver and had an idea a minute," said McLeod. In 1951, the two of them took a trip together to the Okanagan where Tong was going to open a cash-and-carry store, a wholesale outlet that would allow local grocery stores, restaurants and farmers to drop by and shop for supplies, pay cash, and carry goods away just like a consumer in a retail store.

"Tong was pretty excited about the project," said McLeod. "He talked about it and a dozen other

possibilities he was considering, all the way to Penticton. When he wasn't talking business he was talking baseball. The cash-and-carry outlet was a big success; it went strong for 10 years and then union problems closed it down."

It was Tong's unique talent to remain affable and outwardly easygoing while focussing intensely on expanding the family business. His objective was to carry on with his father's vision of building H.Y. Louie into a major player and he admitted no other personal ambition or goal. With the same unassuming boldness with which he moved his residence into a white neighbourhood, he personally inserted himself into the city's business mainstream. When it was still unusual for a Chinese man to join the Vancouver Board of Trade, Tong established himself in the Junior Board of Trade and used it as a stepping stone to active membership. He also joined the YMCA, in those early years the domain of white businessmen on the way up. Once a member, he exercised and engaged in the sports programs on a regular basis, something he would do until the year he died.

Tong's reason for joining trade organizations was the usual one, to associate with other businessmen, but with added emphasis because of his isolation from the mainstream. As soon as the company could afford it, he took part in the Board of Trade's business junkets, rarely missing a trip in all his years as a member. He joined the Canadian Wholesale Grocery Association (CWGA), and ultimately became one of its governors. Once he joined any of these organizations, he became an active participant, attending conventions, taking part in events and serving on executives.

Charles Trimble first met Tong in a warehouse in Oklahoma City during an event hosted by the National American Wholesale Grocers Association.

"We were to study the latest techniques and systems used in the grocery distribution area," said Trimble. "I had heard of Tong Louie. My first impression of him was that he was a relaxed, friendly, approachable individual . . . and that he was there to learn all he could."

At the time, Tong's involvement in these organizations was unusual. The tendency of most Chinese-Canadian businessmen in the post-war period was to remain insular. Discrimination was no longer as overt as it had been, but it was still there and attempting to penetrate the circle of white commerce carried a risk. This was where Tong made his unique contribution.

Without fanfare but with nerves of steel, he stepped out into the full glare of the business world, gambling that in time he would be accepted.

Through all this he maintained his friendships and business associations in the Chinese community. When a Chinese Golf Club got going in 1950, Tong joined up, linking up with a group of 12 members known as the Three-Four Club. They spent many weekends playing rounds and entering the club's tournaments, though his score was rarely impressive.

TONG LOVED TRAVEL, BUT FOUND IT HARD TO TEAR HIMSELF AWAY FROM BUSINESS. THE VANCOUVER BOARD OF TRADE'S OVERSEAS TRADE MISSIONS COMBINED THE TWO, AND TONG BECAME A REGULAR PARTICIPANT.

"Over the years most or all of us won a trophy," said John Lowe, another member of the club. "But not Tong. We had to create a Never Won Trophy, which we presented to him on a suitable occasion."

He and some of his golf buddies went on to found the Vancouver Chinatown Lions Club in 1954, of which he was second president. The 26 original members of the Chinatown Lions all came from professional and business backgrounds, and in addition to Tong and Tim, included Andrew Lam, the first Canadian-born Chinese pastor, and George D. Wong, the first Chinese manager of a Canadian bank. Over the years, the club raised and donated money to a number of causes in their community from the arts to health care centres.

While Tong was busy travelling around the country, networking and expanding his family's business, his children were growing up.

"I don't have any clear memories of my dad before I was five or six," said Brandt, "but my first recollection was that he came home very late for dinner when he was in town. We used to wait for supper for him until finally, my mother would feed us and then cook another meal for my dad. He would arrive home late and tired. If we were still awake he would come in to see us. He'd try to spend quality time with his family, but it wasn't easy. Now that I am in a similar situation I know how difficult it can be."

The challenge for Tong was to figure out how to combine business and parenting. He made an effort to be a good father, but was away from his family on many occasions. Kurt, three years younger than Brandt, remembers his father playing catch with him on summer evenings, and attending the odd Little League game. "Sometimes I used to caddy for him when he played golf," he said, "but he was gone a lot of the time."

Tong found time to take his wife and family on summer trips, in a car usually, to places like Barkerville,

Yellowstone, Yosemite and other popular vacation spots. Both boys remember, with a certain amount of amusement, a fishing trip they went on to Parksville on Vancouver Island.

"Dad took the two of us out in a rented boat to introduce us to salmon fishing," said Brandt. "We hadn't been out on the waves long when Kurt got seasick. Dad had to bring us back to shore and carry Kurt up to the beach in a very delicate condition. That put an end to fishing.

"On the same trip he took us golfing; we were the caddies. On one hole he asked for a nine iron. I gave him a six iron by mistake and he didn't do very well on that hole. I learned the difference between six and nine the hard way."

Tong was not a strict disciplinarian. As had been the case with his parents, he left Geraldine mostly in charge of raising their children, while he looked after the business. This was partially because of tradition, but also because he was away so much of the time. Another characteristic he shared with his father was a strong belief in the value of education. When he was home he took an avid interest in their schooling.

"He lectured us on the importance of getting good grades," said Kurt. "On those occasions when he came in to say goodnight he would almost always ask how school was going. He was more likely to do this than tell a bedtime story. At the dinner table he might give us a mathematics problem to solve."

Brandt recalls earnest advice on the importance of eating the right foods and getting plenty of exercise. "Under the circumstances he was as good a parent as he was able to be," said Brandt. "It was just that we didn't see enough of him."

Tong's children generally agree that their mother was the most significant parent. "Almost a single parent," observed Brandt. "I would rate her as a caring mother and a remarkable wife. In her own quiet, efficient way she took care of all our problems and, at the same time,

gave my father the support and encouragement he needed to cope with the tremendous demands of the business."

"She was there for us," said Kurt. "She was a great cook. I can still smell her baking. She helped us with our homework and sent us to school with great lunches. The oranges in our lunch bags were always peeled."

"She instilled an appreciation of culture in us," said Brandt, "not in an obvious way, but by a kind of osmosis. She loved the arts as well as new things happening in science and technology, and she managed to pass those feelings on to us."

When Geraldine took the boys to the New York World's Fair she also made certain they visited the city's museums and galleries. In Vancouver, by degrees, she exposed the entire family to both Chinese and Western arts, culture and entertainment.

"There is no doubt about it," said Kurt, "my father ran the show, and he ran it well, but behind him, in quiet, unobtrusive ways, our mother exerted important influences."

Andrea Louie, who later changed her name to Anndraya Luui, was born in 1958, 12 years after Kurt.

She had a slightly different experience growing up and received a different amount of parental attention. Like her brothers though, she would have enjoyed seeing more of her busy father.

Tong attempted to solve this problem by combining business with pleasure. Anndraya remembers travelling to various parts of the country with her mother and father, not for actual holidays but to accompany Tong while he attended trade conventions.

"I can't remember any other delegate to these conventions bringing along a wife and a young child," she said. "My father was trying to kill several birds with one stone, and I didn't experience what might be considered quality time with him. I have to give him marks for trying."

Geraldine did what she could to make these business junkets/family travel events interesting for her young daughter, but there is a certain wistfulness in Anndraya's recollection of those excursions.

"His business was his life by necessity," explained family friend Helen Wong. "There could be no other way. He was torn by this and, in later years, found time to get closer to his family."

CHAPTER 10

Retail—Why Not?

By the late forties H.Y. Louie had finally outgrown the building at 255 E. Georgia that Hok Yat had taken the great leap of faith and mortgaged his future to buy back in 1908. The Louies had since bought and built several adjacent buildings in the same block, but those were no longer enough. Tim looked around for a new space and, in 1950, the company moved to a much bigger warehouse at 615 Taylor Street, on property now occupied by part of the GM Place sports complex. Vancouver's population had risen to 385,000, with 100,000 more in adjacent Burnaby, and another 88,000 across the inlet on the North Shore. Neighbourhood stores multiplied to keep up with this growth and when it came to choosing a supplier, H.Y. Louie was there with its reputation for being reliable and thorough. Regardless of whether the customer was a mom-and-pop corner store or a sprawling grocery emporium, H.Y. Louie provided the same quality of service. Deliveries were on time, the price was right and credit was extended without argument to proprietors who showed reasonable promise of future success.

John Chin, the retired manager of the Produce Terminal, an H.Y. Louie-related company, gives a typical example of the Louies' loyalty to their customers. Chin escaped from Mainland China in 1951, joining his father in Vancouver where he started work in his father's small Chinatown restaurant. Six months later the elder Chin invested in a small cafe and store combination at Fourth Avenue and Alma Street. It was enough of a success that he was able to sell it at a profit three years later and buy a respectable grocery store at 21st and Oak. Named the Tip Top, it catered to some of Vancouver's most prestigious households.

"H.R. MacMillan's wife shopped at our place regularly," said Chin. "So did the wives of other corporation executives. It was a great location."

H.Y. Louie had supplied the Chins with a wide range of products from the first days of the Chinatown restaurant to the acquisition of the Tip Top. "Bill Louie was our contact when we ran the Tip Top," said Chin. "We could call him night and day, any time of the week. H.Y. Louie never let us down."

Success blinded the Chins somewhat, seducing them into buying another grocery store at the corner of Main Street and 25th Avenue. The Pay Low, as it was called, was a different story.

"H.Y. Louie's comptroller warned us against the purchase," admitted Chin, "but we didn't listen to him. When we decided to go for it, H.Y. Louie got behind us and gave us full support, starting with a $10,000 inventory loan, followed by three large truckloads of grocery and produce items to completely stock our shelves. In one week we were in business."

The new location was a disaster. Two years later, Chin sold both stores and joined the H.Y. Louie organization, where he paid back his loan in short order.

"The point is," Chin said, "that H.Y. Louie's policy was to provide for its customers through thick and thin. The word got around."

Vancouver's big wholesalers, as well as organizations much farther away, were now paying close attention to H.Y. Louie's activities.

Not all of Hok Yat's children were interested in the family business. Tim, Tong, Bill and Ernie were the only ones seriously involved, perhaps for the better since different opinions on business methods were kept to a minimum. Even so, there were inevitable differences of approach. Tim, as head of the family and president of the company, had the final authority in all important decisions. As the ultimate guardian of the company's balance sheet he agonized, like his father before him, over cash flow and management of daily operations. His executive responsibilities and the exposed position of the company in the midst of much larger competitors kept him busy with day-to-day problems and short-term decisions.

Tong had a different perspective. His sales trips got him out into the world where he could view the family business from a distance, and he picked up fresh ideas from the trade organizations he belonged to and from the business contacts he cultivated. He took in everything he saw, and spent the long hours between calls turning the clues over in his mind, applying the long-term vision he inherited from his father.

Tim could point with satisfaction at an increase of business every quarter, but Tong was becoming aware of a changing pattern in the food business, one that called for new strategies. Most of H.Y. Louie's grocery store customers were small and medium-sized markets, many of them offering basic foodstuffs. Tong sensed this style of shopping was being pushed aside. He was aware that the new concept of the one-stop supermarket had proven itself in the United States and would soon be spreading across Canada. People liked the concept of a single shopping place where they could purchase everything on their grocery list. They were also paying more attention to pre-packaged foods carrying recognized brands and responding to brand-name chain stores supported by promotional campaigns in the major media. Big business was moving in on the neighbourhood grocery store.

While Tim was prepared to listen to his brother's arguments for a change of approach, he took comfort in the company's improving bottom line and remained convinced that the best plan was to continue building the business by slow degrees following the proven prescription of good service and good products.

In 1951, Donald Grimes, the president of the US-based Independent Grocers Alliance, more widely known as IGA, paid the Louies a visit. IGA was a successful franchising organization, allowing established neighbourhood grocers to meet the big company challenge by providing the high-profile merchandising expertise and purchasing clout of a chain while retaining independent ownership. It had been founded in 1926 by Chicago accountant J. Frank Grimes to compete with chain stores that were threatening his clientele of small independent grocers. By 1930 there were 10,000 IGA stores in 37 states.

The IGA didn't come to Canada until 1951 when Ray Wolfe of Oshawa Wholesale Ltd. obtained the IGA franchising licence for southern Ontario, signing up 150 stores. Encouraged, it was now intent on doing the same thing in western Canada. What it needed was an established wholesaler with access to a large retail grocery store clientele. Kelly Douglas, the leading BC wholesaler, had their own group of voluntary independents and, apparently, none of the other big wholesalers was interested. H.Y. Louie was a small operator, but IGA believed it could fill the bill.

If Tim saw the advantages of representing IGA in British Columbia, he was not sufficiently impressed.

Tong was more open to the idea, seeing it as an opportunity to consolidate the independent grocers, bolster them against the coming supermarket competition, and strengthen H.Y. Louie's position well into the future. After much discussion among the brothers, it was decided that the company was not sufficiently organized or financed to accept the IGA proposal. Grimes left, but he had planted a seed.

The more Tong thought about it, the more convinced he became that joining with IGA was the right move. It meant extending the company well beyond the comfort zone they had been used to. Up to this stage H.Y. Louie was still reliant on the Chinese

GOING FISHIN': ERNIE, WILLIS AND JOHN LOUIE TAKE A BREAK FROM WAREHOUSE DUTIES WITH JOHN LOWE IN 1941.

IGA CAME TO CANADA. THE NEW
"SUPER MARKET" APPROACH WAS
A HIT WITH SHOPPERS ACROSS
THE COUNTRY.

community for its core market. This limited its scope but also gave it great stability. To take on the IGA chain would mean leaving this comfortable niche market behind and going head-to-head with the heavyweights in the mainstream market. It also meant leaving the known world of wholesaling for the unknown territory of retailing. It was daunting, but Tong feared the alternative was to see H.Y. Louie dwindle to a nonentity, lost in a world where large wholesalers, in combination with their own supermarket chains, ruled the food industry. In 1954, Kelly Douglas began to set up its own chain of one-stop supermarkets under the name of SuperValu. Safeway, the American grocery chain, had already been active in BC for years.

When Grimes approached H.Y. Louie again four years later in 1955, his persuasive powers, aligned with the obvious success of the SuperValu chain and Tong's enthusiasm, secured Tim's agreement to venture into the world of retail. Grimes returned to the United States with a signed contract and H.Y. Louie became the franchiser for the Independent Grocers Alliance in BC.

The Louie brothers hurled themselves into the new and unfamiliar business, determined to make it work. IGA did not leave them drifting. Within weeks they sent one of their top franchise experts, Hank Langenberger, to assist in the recruitment of franchise members. Back in Oshawa, Ray Wolfe, one of the principals in IGA's Canadian operations, extended every resource to keep the newcomers afloat.

"We would have been lost without them," said Tong, "but then they had been through all of it before and knew exactly how to proceed. We were rank amateurs and we couldn't afford to stay that way for long."

By the time the Louies joined with IGA, Kelly Douglas was well advanced in the establishment of its supermarket chain. This head start had enabled the big wholesaler to secure some of the most favoured locations in the Vancouver area. Tong and his colleagues had to sort through what was left over.

By joining **IGA**, neighbourhood
stores got the profile of a
brand known across North
America.

"Our choices were limited," he said. "We took the usual guidelines into account; the location of the existing store, the volume of sales, evidence of good management and efficiency. I knew most of the owners we were dealing with because H.Y. Louie had been supplying them for years, and that helped in assessing them. We selected the ones that seemed most suited to the IGA system and then we made our approach."

It was slow going at first. Store owners had to be convinced that their businesses would improve under the IGA umbrella. Part of Tong's task was to persuade them to relinquish old, familiar methods of doing business and adopt the more modern and standardized IGA approach. In some cases loans and other inducements were offered to help persuade them to get with the program. In one respect, Kelly Douglas' earlier establishment of a supermarket chain worked to their advantage. Tong's prospective franchisees were able to see the market share SuperValu was gobbling up and draw an obvious conclusion about what would happen if they didn't do something to compete.

H.Y. Louie's venture into the world of retail proved to be the right strategy at the right time. Vancouver's "village" mentality was fading fast. Following the infusion of new arrivals in the war years, the city's population continued to climb as the newcomers spread word of the region's natural attractions and economic potential. There were refugees from Europe and other war-torn parts of the world and war brides of Canadian servicemen. People also migrated from eastern Canada and the Prairies to this west coast lotus land where snow was rare and jobs were plentiful. In 1954, Vancouver hosted the British Empire Games, highlighted by the historic race between Roger Bannister and John Landy, dubbed the "miracle mile" because it was the first time two milers had broken the four-minute barrier in one outing. The eyes of the world were on that event and the city, and the province received even more international attention.

As president, Tim remained in nominal charge of the new operations, torn between his instinct for caution and the euphoria generated by the venture. Tong was the moving force, inspired by his conviction that the IGA decision was the right one, and by his swift and total immersion in the IGA system. Together with Langenberger he surveyed the roster of available stores.

Appealing to the Housewives of North America

Back in the 1950s, when IGA was new to Canadians, things were a little different then they are now. For one thing, grocery prices have changed. Back in 1951, when it was primarily men who supported their families on salaries of $200 to $300 a month, IGA proudly boasted that its stores all strove toward one objective: "to bring the housewives of North America better foods AT LOWER PRICES."

A new car cost a whopping $1,600, but those housewives lucky enough to be able to drive to their local IGA could fill their trunks with coffee that cost just 92 cents a package, jars of jam for 45 cents, and a dozen Arizona oranges for a mere 35 cents.

Of course, back then prices in general were much lower than they are today, but still, it's fun to imagine buying a jar of peanut butter and a loaf of bread for two dimes. The following is the average price of basic food items in Canada in 1951 as priced by the Dominion Bureau of Statistics, precursor to Statistics Canada:

Bread (1 lb. loaf)	12 cents
Peanut Butter (18 oz. jar)	8 cents
Pickles (16 oz. jar)	32 cents
Coffee (reg. 1 lb.)	$1.02
Sugar (1 lb.)	12 cents
Canned Apple Juice (20 oz.)	12 cents
Apples (1 lb.)	11 cents
Grapefruit (half a dozen)	46 cents
Tomatoes (1 lb.)	25 cents
Lettuce (1 lb.)	18 cents
Canned Peas (15 oz.)	16 cents
Eggs (1 doz.)	72 cents
Butter (1 lb.)	68 cents
Milk (1 qt.)	20 cents
Hamburger (1 lb.)	68 cents
Pork Sausage (1 lb)	50 cents
Bologna (1 lb.)	50 cents
Canned Salmon (8 oz.)	26 cents
Cake Mix (14 oz. pkg.)	5 cents

When you convert the imperial measurements to metric and multiply the prices by 10 to get a comparable price to what we would pay today, suddenly the 1950s' prices no longer seem so reasonable. Can you imagine spending $7.20 or more on a carton of eggs?

Restaurants began serving alcoholic beverages with food and television started stealing audiences from sports events and movie houses. Tong's old friend, Arthur Laing, already a successful politician at the provincial level, had gone on to win a federal seat in 1952. With him went Douglas Jung, a young lawyer who had taken full advantage of the franchise granted to the Chinese in 1947, thrown his hat into the political ring and won, becoming Canada's first Chinese-Canadian MP. The Social Credit, a fledgling political party led by the inimitable W.A.C. (Wacky) Bennett, had slid past its CCF rivals and was now in provincial command. Bennett was a builder extraordinaire.

JOYCE BUNKA WORKED AS A SWITCHBOARD OPERATOR AT THE H.Y. LOUIE BUILDING ON TAYLOR STREET FOR YEARS.

Highways, bridges, dams and railways proliferated, all made possible by the post-war boom.

In this supercharged atmosphere, an increasingly sophisticated and eclectic population demanded more elaborate services throughout the economy. By 1956, Tong had succeeded in franchising 20 independent grocery stores, all of which experienced improved sales thanks to their upgrading by IGA.

In 1957, Dominion Stores, a large eastern Canadian food chain, decided to move into the Vancouver market, arriving with a flourish and winning over many city shoppers. Their supermarkets were spacious, bright and well stocked. They offered a wide choice of groceries, meats and produce, plus innovative in-store bakeries, delis, and cafeterias for the foot weary. This formidable intruder could spell nothing but trouble for IGA and its relatively modest outlets. At least this seemed to be the case until Dominion Stores decided to use H.Y. Louie as their supplemental wholesale source, principally because they were not connected with the competing supermarket chains. It was an enormous step up for the company. Not only was it supplying the IGA chain and hundreds of independents, it was now a principal supplier to Dominion's state-of-the-art supermarkets. The Louies could now be counted in with the other big boys on the wholesale block, if not among the very largest.

Never one to ignore new products and merchandising techniques, Tong tried, and often succeeded, in persuading Tim to test the market with items that had shown promise elsewhere. At this time, no stores carried any frozen foods to speak of. Frozen food was coming into use, but it was mainly sold and stored by special services known as frozen food "lockers." Prior to the early 1950s, most households did not have their own home freezers, so they had to keep their frozen goods—usually bulk items like sides of beef—at these central community freezers. Tong foresaw the trend to home freezers and was the first to stock pre-packaged

frozen food products in retail stores, an innovation the large chains resisted until enthusiastic public response proved it worked. Then all of them installed freezer sections. Tong was often a trendsetter, though he had never taken a formal course in marketing or merchandising.

"I simply didn't have that kind of time," he said. "Whatever I acquired along those lines was picked up at conventions, industry exhibitions and seminars, association lunches and dinners. It was very informal, but it wasn't a bad way to do it. I met new people, made valuable contacts and collected useful ideas. Along the way I was able to witness trends occurring in other parts of the country and the world, and adapt some of them to our business."

As soon as H.Y. Louie became involved in the retail grocery business Tong joined the Food Industry Association of Canada.

As the IGA network expanded, Tim decided to invest in an IGA retail outlet of his own. Together with a partner, he purchased and stocked an IGA store at 49th and Oak and personally entered the world of retail. It was a disappointing experience. The store ran into trouble and incurred considerable debt, undoubtedly justifying his worst fears about the IGA move. While this appears to have dampened his enthusiasm for the business, Tong remained determined to make the venture succeed. Friction began to develop between the two. Tong thought about nothing but the grocery wholesale business, night and day. It was his life and the hours he put in rivalled the effort of his father in the early days. Tim, on the other hand, had distractions. He had become a recognized figure in the Chinese business community and was spending a good deal of his time on community activities. He also had his private interests consisting of the store and

IN 1957 DOMINION STORES, A LARGE ONTARIO-BASED SUPERMARKET CHAIN, MOVED INTO THE VANCOUVER MARKET. IT LOOKED LIKE BAD NEWS UNTIL DOMINION SELECTED H.Y. LOUIE CO. LIMITED AS THEIR LOCAL WHOLESALER.

some early involvement in the investment business. H.Y. Louie was not his only focus, yet he retained absolute authority over management decisions. H.Y. Louie was everything to Tong, and he had growing ambitions for it he was unable to pursue because he had to get Tim's approval, something he couldn't always do. Now Tim's financial difficulty added to the complexity of the situation. His IGA store had run up considerable debts with H.Y. Louie that were not being paid.

Growing increasingly impatient with the situation, Tong made a dramatic move. With Tim's knowledge, but hardly his blessing, Tong arranged bank financing for a buyout then met with each of his brothers and sisters in turn, explained his reasons, and invited them to sell him their shares in the business. The majority agreed.

Willis was one of those who sold, and for him it was a simple decision. He had worked in the family firm since he was a small boy but didn't see a future for himself at H.Y. Louie because it was still struggling and he didn't think there was room for all of them. He was happy to cash out and start his own career, and others presumably felt the same. Willis went into the insurance business, first working for a leading commercial agency, then starting his own successful agency.

Having secured voting control of the company, Tong was still faced with the sensitive task of negotiating the turnover of executive powers with his older brother. As an inducement, Tong offered to retire Tim's IGA debt in exchange for his shares. The debt was in the $80,000 area and the shares were valued at $38,000, so it was an attractive offer.

The result was that Tim stepped down and Tong assumed control of H.Y. Louie. It would be wrong to say the changeover occurred without stirring some feelings of resentment and regret, but it was conducted with a minimum of contention and Tim went on to a successful career in the investment business.

THE CHEERY INTERIOR OF AN EARLY **IGA** STORE. INDEPENDENT GROCERS WHO JOINED **IGA** BENEFITED FROM NATIONAL MARKETING AND PROMOTIONAL CAMPAIGNS THEY COULD NEVER HAVE AFFORDED ON THEIR OWN, GIVING THEM A CHANCE AGAINST THE BIG CHAINS.

TONG HAVING A GOOD TIME WITH
SALESMEN **DICK WALKER** AND
GARY MACDONALD AT AN
H.Y. LOUIE CHRISTMAS
PARTY IN **1959.**

CHAPTER 11

Shopping for Supermarkets

In retrospect it is clear that in taking over direction of H.Y. Louie, Tong was only doing what he saw he must do in order to transform the family firm into a major corporation. Since we know that he succeeded, it is easy to underestimate what an audacious act it was. It is always easy to underestimate the achievement of a visionary who turns out to be right. What we have to remember is that in replacing his elder brother Tong was challenging one of the most deeply-rooted Chinese traditions, that of primogeniture. But he had the insight to understand that in the new world he was born into, making the most of an opportunity was more important than observing an old custom. He had the insight, and he had the nerve to act on it. He had these qualities to a degree that set him apart from all but a handful of his contemporaries. This showed up not just in the fact that he took over the company, but in the calm and confident way he went about it.

Grant Hammond, a retired partner in the accounting firm of Deloitte & Touche, first met Tong in 1961 as the senior auditor on the H.Y. Louie account. "Tong had taken over from his brother Tim

not too much earlier," he said. "Major administrative changes had occurred and it might have been expected that the company would be in some kind of disarray. That was not my impression. Tong seemed to have a firm grip on things. As an auditor coming in from the outside, you pick up vibrations. As the saying goes, I sensed no bad vibes, although I was aware that uncomfortable relations existed between Tong and Tim."

Tong immediately impressed Hammond with his friendliness and openness. "Tong Louie demonstrated absolutely no pretensions. He gave the impression that he knew where he was going and how to get there. Not only was he available to talk to me, he was genuinely interested in what I had to say, and was quite frank in divulging some of the plans for the company."

In 1967 the Louies moved a few blocks to a larger house at Southlands Place where his sons and daughter, under Geraldine's guidance, finished growing up. During this time, Tong dedicated himself to increasing the IGA franchise membership and building the H.Y. Louie wholesale infrastructure to keep pace with the growing list of stores. Not all was smooth sailing. As could be expected, the other retail

chains remained fiercely competitive. Even within the ranks of Dominion Stores, where H.Y. Louie's position might have seemed secure, problems arose. Ever in search of better ways to serve his large array of retail grocery accounts, Tong branched out even further into frozen foods. He had initiated this business on a smaller scale earlier, and when it succeeded, he began concentrating on it in earnest. Nationally, Dominion Stores had contracted to purchase all of its frozen food products from Ruby Distributors. Regardless, Tong pressed Dominion Stores in BC to stock H.Y. Louie frozen foods at better prices and with quicker service. The Dominion Stores' merchandising manager in Vancouver knew a good deal when he saw it and began to buy frozen foods from H.Y. Louie, reducing Ruby Distributors' share of the market.

This didn't last long. Ruby Distributors, stung by Tong's aggressive tactics, confronted Dominion Stores' head office people in Toronto and demanded that Dominion live up to its contract. The result was that the BC stores were ordered to stop purchasing frozen foods from H.Y. Louie immediately.

As Dominion was their largest market for frozen foods, this was a severe blow to H.Y. Louie and Tong resisted it strenuously—offering more attractive price inducements and cajoling as best he could—to no avail. As the then merchandising manager for Dominion in BC, Ed Hellinger had the job of cutting Tong off.

"Tong came up fighting and challenged me on the decision," said Hellinger. "(He was) extremely determined in achieving his objectives—always give it another try, and another, and another." But the decision was not Hellinger's to change. Tong lost the battle and retreated to a minor position in the frozen food field for the next few years.

Possibly because Dominion Stores had entered the field too late to overtake the SuperValus and other food chains now firmly in place, such as Safeway, the

CHINATOWN WAS A CHEERFUL PLACE BY 1960, THE NEON SIGNS OF PENDER STREET A MAGNET FOR VANCOUVERITES OF ALL BACKGROUNDS.

company was having difficulty capturing its anticipated share of market. In 1968, it decided to cut its losses and pull out of BC. Suddenly there were nine, large, modern supermarkets available for purchase. Tong was invited to enter the first offer.

Tong's accountants and business associates cautioned him that the Dominion Stores acquisition would be unwise. If Dominion couldn't succeed in British Columbia how did Tong expect to? In running the IGA franchising business H.Y. Louie was in the position of guiding and supporting retailers but that was far different from actually owning and operating their own retail chain. That was a whole different ballgame, and one into which Tong would have to plunge headlong if he took on the extensive Dominion property. Tong heard a dozen convincing reasons against the acquisition and few for it. The most compelling came from his chief financial backer, the Royal Bank, which not only refused to finance the deal but warned him not to spend a nickel of H.Y. Louie's existing line of credit supporting the venture. He weighed all the advice respectfully, then opted to purchase the stores. Now H.Y. Louie owned supermarkets of the first magnitude and Tong was in the retail business for real.

A very perilous challenge was now confronting H.Y. Louie. This is the passage from family firm to corporation; from a stage where it can be effectively run in a hands-on way by the founder to the next stage where it must be run by a management team following a corporate program. The main pitfall is that the founders fail to delegate executive control, overburdening themselves and creating a leadership failure at the top. Tong was an ideal candidate to fall into this because he had a strong tendency—shared with Tim before him, and certainly with his father before that—to direct operations single-handedly. They were all keenly entrepreneurial, but the entrepreneurial impulse is no rarer than the managerial touch. Having both qualities together in elite form is an almost surefire formula for

ALTHOUGH HIS BANK REFUSED TO LEND HIM THE MONEY AND HIS ACCOUNTANTS WARNED HIM AGAINST IT, IN 1968 TONG DECIDED TO ACQUIRE DOMINION'S NINE BC STORES AND OPERATE THEM UNDER THE IGA FLAG. THEIR SUCCESS TRIGGERED A QUANTUM LEAP FORWARD FOR H.Y. LOUIE CO. LIMITED IN THE EARLY 1970S.

AN H.Y. LOUIE FUNCTION IN
MARCH 1964. IN THE REAR IS
ANDY YIP, JOHN AND LIL LOWE,
GARY AND FRANKIE MACDONALD,
WITH MRS. ANDY YIP, AILEEN AND
BILL SHARNELL IN THE FRONT ROW.

success in the business world. It was at this critical juncture Tong showed himself to have these extraordinary qualifications.

Although it was difficult for him to step back, he realized that the company had grown to a size and complexity that made ruling alone impossible. He saw specifically that the management of large supermarkets called for expertise he lacked, and moved to entice key Dominion Store personnel into joining H.Y. Louie before they could migrate back to head office in eastern Canada. One of the first he headhunted was the man who had stonewalled him when he was trying to win back his frozen food business—Dominion's merchandizing manager, Ed Hellinger. He came aboard as retail operations manager and stayed with Tong until he retired almost 23 years later. Tong also kept operational staff intact. On March 12, 1968, he reported that 235 of the 297 persons employed by Dominion

had been rehired by H.Y. Louie. As a result, the transition from Dominion to IGA was relatively smooth.

When the delegation of responsibilities become a must, Tong grew adept at it, promoting and delegating within the ranks of his own organization while keeping his eyes open for promising candidates within the industry. Another key element of his executive skill set was that ability to recognize and recruit management talent, which sets the best CEOs apart. He chose his people carefully, dealt with them on a one-to-one basis, expected much of them and rewarded them commensurately. With competent managers in place he was able to find more breathing space. In his own way he relaxed a bit—although his management style just shifted from being all-consuming to being in close liaison with his managers. He always kept his door open to all levels of the companies. It was not in his nature to pull rank, although his authority was never questioned.

He gave them the freedom to exercise their abilities to the fullest and they shared the load with him, relieving him of much of the pressure of running the business on a day-to-day basis.

When Grant Hammond first met Tong, he quickly realized Tong demanded openness, directness and honesty. "Later I observed these same requirements applied to the strong management structure he put in place," said the auditor.

Ed Hellinger believes Tong developed wisdom from having gone through hard times. And while experiences like toughing out the Depression may have instilled good survival instincts, they also sometimes made life more difficult for his managers.

"Things were not easy for any of us after the Dominion Stores acquisition," said Hellinger. "Adapting to a much larger operation created financial stress that didn't abate until the early '70s when the picture improved.

"We often had difficulty persuading him to upgrade, modernize or advertise. He had always operated on a 'bare bones' basis and it was difficult to get

BY KEEPING THE WELL-TRAINED DOMINION STAFF, TONG ENSURED A SMOOTH TRANSITION WHEN HE TOOK OVER THE NINE WEST COAST SUPERMARKETS.

WEEK'S OF TRAINING on Dominion's "More Friendly" policy and economical prices have prepared a skilled corps of cashiers to give efficient service at the new market. Manager Howard Smith is teacher.

TONG WAS ABLE TO KEEP **235** OF THE **297** DOMINION STAFF WHEN HE ACQUIRED THE LARGE-FORMAT STORES.

A TYPICAL **H.Y.** LOUIE INVOICE—
BEFORE THE COMPUTER AGE.

him to invest in what he considered to be non-essentials and trappings. I think this was a carry-over from his early life when every penny had to be accounted for. He had a fundamental dislike for any signs of waste or conspicuous consumption."

Dealing with other business people he was fair but firm. "One does not earn the reputation he earned by being a softie or a vacillator."

Mel Cooper, later chairman of CFAX Radio in Victoria, remembers his first encounter with Tong Louie.

"My dad ran a grocery store," he said, "but I wasn't interested in following in his footsteps. Instead I decided to try my hand at radio sales and marketing. One of my first assignments was to tackle the H.Y. Louie Company. I made preliminary advertising presentations to Bill and Ernie Louie who were quite receptive, although they warned me that the final decision was up to their brother, Tong, and that he was very conservative where advertising was concerned.

"The day came when I had to present to Tong Louie. He was seated at his desk with a stack of correspondence in front of him, and I lost his attention within minutes of starting my pitch. When he picked up a letter, I stopped talking until he focussed on me again. The stop/start game went on for some time until finally he settled back in his chair and said, 'Okay, Mr. Cooper, I get the message.' Fifteen minutes later he signed my first IGA contract."

The signature came with an admonition, however. "I'm giving you a try because you're Ron Cooper's son," he said, "and I respect him as a person. If we have a

H.Y. LOUIE WAREHOUSE EMPLOYEE LARRY CHANG PUNCHES OUT ON THE TIME CLOCK.

second meeting it will depend on you and what you're made of."

Cooper and Louie became close friends in the following years. "He treated me with a fatherly approach," Cooper said, "handing out advice when he thought it necessary. He placed great importance on a good reputation. 'It's a person's most important asset,' he told me more than once."

Tong enjoyed a good reputation with his staff, although he sometimes placed them under enormous pressure. Ed Hellinger confirmed Tong as being an exceptional visionary. "When driven by some kind of instinct, he explored the possibilities as far as he could to satisfy himself that he was on the track of an achievable objective. Then he committed to the idea and followed up with whatever was needed to turn it

LARRY CHANG AT THE WHEEL
OF AN H.Y. LOUIE DELIVERY TRUCK
IN 1970.

into successful reality. At this point he took risks, but they were carefully calculated risks."

Tong remained focussed on making his business succeed far into the future and this influenced almost his every move.

"Characteristically the man always thought in the long term," said Hellinger. "I heard him use the expression hundreds of times in all kinds of situations. He had little time or patience for any plan that had no long-term potential or value. Once he set the parameters of a new business plan he left the details to those he assigned to carry them out.

"To my corporately trained business mind his approach to business sometimes frightened me. It took time to accept that his ways were often better for our business than the stiff, conventional approach of big organizations."

As a boss, he says Tong inspired loyalty by demonstrating loyalty himself and always keeping his word. He refused to carry a grudge or berate his people after he pointed out their errors. If Hellinger had any criticism, it related to Tong's performance acknowledgment—or rather, his lack thereof.

"All of us who worked for him always wished for better feedback from him during or after a major task or project. Perhaps it was his sensitivity for the judgment of others that kept him from imposing his own judgment. He was a good listener and an equally good judge of what he heard.

"I admired the man tremendously," he said. "In spite of my business training and experience, I learned a lot from him and he was a very patient teacher. One of my strongest first impressions of him was of his loyalty to his family, employees and franchisees. Next would be his modesty concerning himself, which has now become legendary."

THE INDEFATIGABLE LARRY CHANG MOVES A BIG STACK OF JUICE CARTONS IN THE H.Y. LOUIE WAREHOUSE ON TAYLOR STREET.

CHAPTER 12

Warning from Within

The period following the acquisition of Dominion Stores was a busy one. The IGA chain continued to expand under the direction of Tong, who was ostensibly exerting his command through his management infrastructure but was never far removed from the main action. Tong—far from the days when he was blackballed by BC Sugar for retailing a small bag of sugar—now moved comfortably between the worlds of wholesaling and retailing. He had endured the worst his competition could hand him and was no longer at the mercy of the other wholesalers. He had done an end run around them by consolidating a bloc of major retail outlets that were dedicated to H.Y. Louie as their supplier.

The IGA system turned out to be very effective for this purpose. Kelly Douglas, Safeway and others favoured a policy of establishing company-owned stores, which had the advantage of greater control but limited the number of stores they could afford to build and manage in a given period. The cost of setting up new stores and building new clientele also limited them to the higher traffic venues, mostly new shopping centres, where such major installations could be justified. There were only so many such locations available at any given time. The IGA franchising system allowed Tong to get stores into the H.Y. Louie shopping cart without actually having to purchase them or manage them directly. Because of the comparatively low set-up cost of franchising and the fact they were absorbing going concerns, Tong was able to sign up the smaller neighbourhood stores.

As more mid-sized independents felt the pressure of the chains with their high profiles and intensive marketing, they turned for help to their old friend Tong, who had been cheerfully calling on them since he drove a Model A. Tong had the perfect solution for them. By bringing them into the IGA group, he could give them the profile of a brand known across North America, give them the benefit of his group's strong promotional activities, improve their selection and merchandising, and help them keep local shoppers buying in their old neighbourhoods. In promoting this approach Tong was pursuing two principles he strongly believed in. First was the importance of the community, and second was the power of individual entrepreneurship. He knew from personal experience how hard the small family business person would struggle to survive, and he was happy to be in a position to strengthen their hand, especially since so many were personal friends. He knew every corner of the province from his years as a travelling sales rep for H.Y. Louie and used his knowledge to give IGA franchises broad distribution throughout rural BC.

While the emphasis on neighbourhood shopping was central to the IGA strategy in BC and has remained so ever since, Tong was careful not to get shut out of the more centralized shopping centre market. Using his flagship ex-Dominion supermarkets as a base, he continued to develop larger-format stores in new malls, mostly in partnership with independent

LEWIS' IGA IN NANAIMO WAS ONE OF THE STORES TONG SIGNED UP IN THE 1950S.

developers and managers. Often the new owners were members of the families whose parents H.Y. Louie had been associated with for years, as the firm continued to build on its old network of loyal affiliations. It was said about H.Y. Louie—and still is—that if you played ball with the company and got accepted into the IGA business family, it would look after you. It was Hok Yat's old philosophy of treating people as the most valuable resource, still going strong.

Tong's strategy allowed IGA to take in a much broader spectrum of stores than the competing chains. It also took less capital, management resources and time than the "company store" approach, allowing H.Y. Louie to gain control of a much larger slice of the retail market than it could have otherwise. And it all had the result of capturing a larger share of the province's wholesale grocery business for H.Y. Louie. Tong's masterful game plan ended by vaulting H.Y. Louie over the heads of his old competitors into the top rank of West Coast food wholesalers.

Willis Louie pinpoints the 1968–1974 period as the one in which H.Y. Louie finally arrived as a successful corporation and gave its owners some financial comfort for the first time. He remembers Tong saying one of the senior officers from the Royal Bank formally apologized for not having sufficient faith in his judgment when they refused to finance the Dominion takeover. "They said to him, 'Don't hold it against us. Next time you have a deal, come to us and we'll make up for it.'"

Tong was not one to misplace an I.O.U. like that.

With the business now doing well and a good management team in place, Tong had more time to expend in other directions. He took advantage of more trade conventions and the travel they entailed, to the point that the Vancouver Board of Trade's overseas trade missions became an unfailing part of his annual itinerary. Being business-oriented, these trips allowed Tong to travel with a clear conscience and he enjoyed

HIS RELIABILITY AND INTEGRITY WON TONG A HIGH DEGREE OF LOYALTY FROM IGA FRANCHISEES. BY THE MID-1970S THE SMALL-IS-BETTER APPROACH BEGAN TO PAY OFF AS H.Y. LOUIE MOVED INTO THE FRONT RANK OF WEST COAST WHOLESALERS.

THE VANCOUVER BOARD OF TRADE'S OVERSEAS MISSIONS BECAME A FAVOURITE PART OF TONG'S ANNUAL ROUTINE. HERE DELEGATES VISIT MITSUBISHI'S SHIPYARD AND ENGINE WORKS IN KOBE, JAPAN.

them immensely. Whenever possible he took Geraldine along.

As Ed Hellinger explained, Tong never got used to spending money. "Tong was always thrifty," he said. "He disliked signs of waste, or display or conspicuous consumption." Occasionally, however, he didn't feel the need to justify his travels. In 1969, when he was 55, he met his old friend Dr. Fred Chu for lunch.

"Perhaps it was spring fever that got him started," said Chu, "but he had a proposition for me. In his opinion we were getting on in years ... He proposed that we take a trip somewhere while we still had our health. The travel party would consist of me, my wife and 14-year-old son, Tong, his wife and 10-year-old

daughter. It seemed like a great idea to me, I was ready for a holiday, but there was one problem."

Doctor Chu's 17-year-old son would have to be left behind to spend his days unsupervised. Tong came up with a solution. He arranged a summer job for young Gerry Chu in the H.Y. Louie organization. The boy returned to the summer job each year until he entered dentistry at the University of British Columbia. As he did with so many other people in his life, Tong made a point of staying in touch with the younger man. In 1988, while on a business trip to the Okanagan, he took a considerable detour to Salmon Arm to visit Gerry, who by then had a dental practice in the community.

Tong also found relaxation in sports. When he was younger he was active in soccer, track and field, tennis, and later in golf. He continued to follow these sports with keen interest, and stuck to his YMCA routine which, starting in 1960, included a five-kilometre run through Stanley Park. In 1968, he was one of the first Chinese to be granted membership in the Shaughnessy Golf and Country Club, which until then had remained an exclusively white club.

Tong's most reliable method of relaxing, however, was to attach himself to his favourite pipe. This appears to have been a mild addiction, although he displayed no others and even stopped drinking in his forties. His pipe was with him always, during business or pleasure, cold much of the time, but usually in his hand or mouth. There are those among Tong's friends and colleagues who theorize that he used his pipe as a bargaining tool. Faced with a decision or a convoluted proposal, he sucked on his pipe, examined it, lit it once or twice, or did whatever else he could to give himself time to think the problem through.

Anndraya recalls a trip she went on with Tong and Geraldine to the fish ladders at Hell's Gate in the Fraser River Canyon. "I was quite excited," she said. "My mother had prepared me for the sight of big salmon leaping up the fish ladders. We started out in fine style, and then my father discovered that he had left his pipe behind. He couldn't drive without it and turned back to get it. The joy and anticipation of the outing faded away for me."

Colleagues and visitors alike saw Tong, as often as not, tamping his pipe, lighting it, brandishing it to make a point, or holding it suspended as he concentrated on a conversation or business debate. Ed Hellinger, a retired company executive, tells of an airline trip he shared with Tong to an IGA annual meeting in eastern Canada.

"We hadn't been in the air half an hour when Tong reached into his pocket for his pipe, lit it, and settled back in his seat. It was an entirely reflex action. Before I could nudge him, a stewardess came running up and told him, in no uncertain terms, to put his pipe away. Tong was embarrassed and apologized to the passengers near him.

"At the meeting I mentioned the episode to some of the directors and raised a chuckle. However, Ray Wolfe, president of IGA Canada, was also on the board of Canadian Pacific Airlines, and he decided to use some influence. When we boarded the plane to return to Vancouver, Tong got the red carpet treatment. As soon as he was seated, a stewardess approached and told him he could smoke his pipe at any time. I think she would have supplied him with a pipe and tobacco if he had asked. He smiled and thanked her, but he kept his pipe in his pocket."

In 1964 it was decided to divide the Canadian and American IGA operations and IGA Canada Ltd. was formed, wholly owned by its wholesaler shareholders. As an IGA wholesaler H.Y. Louie was entitled to a seat on the IGA board of directors and the position was taken by Tong, the first and possibly most involving of many board positions to come. He eventually graduated to vice-chairman of the board, sharing responsibilities with Al Graham of the Oshawa Group, a large IGA wholesaler serving the Ontario market. Years later, Graham paid tribute to Tong's contribution.

"Tong was the quiet shareholder, who patiently listened to the issues and dealt with them at the appropriate time, and in a gentlemanly manner. Tong was most often the peacemaker between two strong and opposing forces in Ray Wolfe (of the Oshawa Group) and Bert Loeb (of M. Loeb, Inc., a rival Ontario wholesaler). In many respects, Tong's hidden strengths came from an ability to see and stay focussed on the larger picture. I often described Tong as the glue that bound things together."

The acquisition of the Dominion IGA chain and the continuing addition of independent grocery stores to the IGA roster created the need for much larger warehouse facilities. In 1972 H.Y. Louie moved its operations to a new, specially designed structure on Production Way in the Lake City Industrial Park adjacent to the Lougheed Highway in Burnaby. Both administrative offices and warehousing were accommodated in 100,000 square feet of space, with an option on another 100,000 square feet—a far cry from the 25 by 120 foot building in Chinatown where the Louie family had laboured and lived for so long.

In the new complex was one of Tong's few concessions to luxury: a handsomely appointed office, richly carpeted, with a desk equal to any in Canada's towers of power. When visitors expressed their admiration, he would apologize for it.

Kurt observed that his father's biggest indulgence was in the matter of cars, and it was hardly extreme. "He owned a four-barrel, '57 Chevrolet and was very proud of it. In 1963 he indulged himself with an Oldsmobile Starfire convertible, but his new cars were few and far between."

Old friend Helen Wong explained: "He was not fussy about food, clothes or acquisitions. I think his pipe was his most precious possession."

While the years following the association with IGA were marked with steady success, they were not without misfortune. Tong's brother Ernie, who was still deeply involved in the activities of the company and one of his closest confidants, died prematurely in 1971. It was a tremendous blow to the entire family. Ernie had kept some of his shares in H.Y. Louie and stayed in the firm, but his contribution was different from that of his brother Bill. If Bill was the wheelhorse in the back room, Ernie was the court jester. He did his duty, but he tried not to let it get in the way of enjoying life. He was always trying to talk up a party. Every company needs a blithe spirit who can be counted on to keep things from getting too serious, and Ernie

played that role with flair. His bright spirit was tremendously missed by the whole organization. Then, in 1974, on the Norway leg of a Vancouver Board of Trade business tour of European markets, Tong became ill. It began as a cold and then escalated into a flu-like condition, which he battled impatiently. One of his fellow travellers offered him penicillin tablets from his own stash of medications. Tong took them and, within hours, reacted violently to the antibiotic. He became desperately ill and, on the advice of the Norwegian doctors, was flown back to Vancouver for continuing medical attention.

He became weaker every day. Friends who visited him were shocked at his appearance. His robust frame had wasted away, lesions had appeared on his face and body and still he tried to shake it off, believing this illness, like every other challenge in his life, would be overcome by sheer exertion of will.

Even Geraldine's usually persuasive powers couldn't budge his resolve. Finally his son Kurt wore down his resistance. "He wouldn't accept the fact that his condition was critical," said Kurt, "but I think I got to him when his willpower was at its lowest, because he agreed to go to the hospital."

Ed Hellinger said, "His condition was so severe, most of the attending physicians had given him up as gone. He lost his skin several times, as I recall. I visited him in hospital and had difficulty recognizing him. Totally emaciated, he was just a shadow of his former self."

Tong was hospitalized for weeks, during which time his prognosis was grave on several occasions. Had he not been in such good shape to begin with, he would likely have died. Finally he responded to treatment and emerged from hospital atrophied but on the mend. Like his father before him, he had developed full-blown diabetes. Fortunately it was now a much more controllable condition. His father had died when insulin treatment was still in the early stages.

IN 1926 J. FRANK GRIMES founded the Independent Grocers Alliance. Grimes was a Chicago-based accountant who realized that by combining their purchasing power grocers could buy better than individual retailers. That first year, Grimes was able to convince 64 grocers to band together under a banner that would soon be recognizable to customers all across the United States. But it wasn't just people in the United States who liked what Grimes was offering.

In the 1940s Ray Wolfe, the president of the Ontario Produce Company, saw how the alliance improved competition against the growing buying power of the large supermarket chains and decided to bring IGA to Canada. It took him a couple of tries before he was able to secure the IGA franchise he wanted, however. The first time he went to Chicago with a proposal to grant the Ontario Produce Company the first IGA wholesale franchise in Canada he was turned down, ostensibly because his company was not a full-service wholesaler. Not to be deterred, Wolfe bought out Baker's Food Supplies Ltd., changed its name to Oshawa Wholesale Ltd, and went back to Chicago as a full-line wholesaler. He was turned down

again, this time because the US company said it didn't know how it would market IGA in Canada. Wolfe was none too pleased, but being the go-getter he was he reasoned that if the Americans didn't want to start up in Canada, he would start a Canadian version of IGA on his own. He began meeting with willing independent retailers, many of whom were enthusiastic about the IGA concept.

Wind of Wolfe's activities soon made its way down to Chicago where Don Grimes, the son of Frank Grimes, was the IGA's president. Grimes boarded a train north to meet with Wolfe. On September 25, 1950, Wolfe's gutsy move paid off when he signed the papers to be the IGA's franchised wholesaler for Southern Ontario.

In 1951 Wolfe opened Canada's first IGA retail store in Toronto. It was an immediate success and by the end of the year there were 54 other IGA retailers in Ontario with combined sales of nearly $7 million. Three years later the Louie brothers began franchising IGA in British Columbia and within a year convinced 47 grocers to join the franchise. By 2001 there were 600 stores nationwide and sales volumes are approaching $6 billion.

In 1964 IGA's Canadian operations became independent from its US arm although the two remained on friendly terms. Following the separation, the Americans tended to treat the Canadians like a younger brother: they were helpful, but a little paternalistic. But it was IGA Canada that had the foresight to register the IGA trademark in 20 other countries. The result? There are now thousands of stores in places as disparate as Australia, Brazil, Malaysia, Singapore, South Africa, Indonesia, China, Japan and Korea, and when the IGA USA wants to expand into another country it often has to ask for IGA Canada's permission.

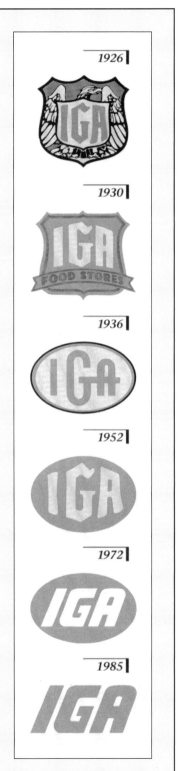

1926

1930

1936

1952

1972

1985

one occurred during his visit with his father to the ancestral village where he took responsibility for carrying out Hok Yat's vision of a family dynasty in the new world; the other occurred during the depths of his near-fatal illness when he faced his own death and realized he had a limited time to do all the things he wanted to do.

Already some of the most important things were falling into place. He had repeated the good fortune of his father in being blessed by worthy heirs. His eldest son, Brandt, had graduated from the University of British Columbia in 1966 with a degree in commerce. After articling with the accounting firm of Touche Ross, he joined the company in 1973, first as a buyer, then as the director of merchandising. It was clear early on that he had inherited his father's executive talent. The dynasty was secure for another generation. Back in his office again Tong was pleased to see that H.Y. Louie had been well managed in his absence, allowing him to resume command with a minimum of stress. Soon he was functioning again at full capacity, a tribute to his exceptional physique and intense willpower.

The premature deaths of his brothers and his own brush with death made Tong conscious of his mortality. He became even more health and fitness conscious than before. The YMCA workout—already a regular part of his routine—became an unbreakable regimen. He exercised and ran in the early morning hours in order to arrive at his office as business began. Although he had seen that H.Y. Louie and IGA could operate without his constant presence, he couldn't relax. He had to consolidate the business operations and secure them in the hands of the next generation. And he had to get on with an interest he had already started—community service. Until this stage of his life he had been focussed on building the means to be charitable, and he was determined to deliver on the second part while he was vital enough to make a good job of it. But first, he was not quite finished building.

Tong's recovery was long and difficult, made more so by his impatience to get on with the job. Added to the troubles of that year was the death of his brother Bill, who with Ernie, had been a pillar of strength in the period following the IGA acquisition. His two family lieutenants were now gone, leaving him alone to guide the family business.

Willis says Bill (called Bew by the family) left particularly large shoes to be filled. "I always say Bew was the unsung hero of H.Y. Louie," says Willis. "He was the one in the back doing most of the work nobody else wanted to do. He really slaved to build that company from the operations side. And then the poor guy died before he could really collect his reward."

Despite the debilitating effects of his illness and his bereavement, Tong never succumbed to depression. Adversity had always been a challenge to him and now he felt supremely challenged. People have turning points in the course of their lives, most of them small and indiscernible except in retrospect. Looking back, Tong was able to identify two significant epiphanies:

ABOVE: THE NEWLY COMPLETED H.Y. LOUIE DISTRIBUTION CENTRE AND OFFICES IN BURNABY IN 1972.

OPPOSITE: BILL LOUIE WITH HIS DAUGHTERS SUSAN AND LAURA. BILL WAS REMEMBERED BY SOME AS THE "UNSUNG HERO OF H.Y. LOUIE" BECAUSE OF HIS DEDICATED EFFORTS BEHIND THE SCENES.

TONG NEVER WENT ANYWHERE
WITHOUT HIS PIPE. FRIENDS
THEORIZED THAT HE USED IT BOTH
FOR RELAXING AND AS A DIVERSION
DURING NEGOTIATIONS.

Prescription for Success

When Sam Bass bought Schoff's old drugstore on Main Street in 1945, renamed it London Drugs, and proceeded to launch what he trumpeted as the first "modern" drugstore in the province, it wasn't long before Tong and everybody else in Vancouver knew about it. Bass was an immigrant farmer's son who managed to pick up a university degree and had a strong entrepreneurial bent, but there all resemblance between him and Tong ended. Bass was as flamboyant and opinionated as Tong was modest and unassuming. He was never happier than when he was out on the street, or in the papers or on the airwaves, beating the publicity drum for his wonderful drugstore. Though two years younger than Tong, Bass succeeded in making himself into one of the city's most recognizable personalities at a time when Tong was still an unknown grocery salesman spending two weeks of the month driving around the province and trying to find time to spend with his young family.

It was a bit of a comedown to actually visit Bass's cramped 1,000 sq. ft. emporium in the depressed east end of the city. Considering all the noise he made about it you might have thought it was a megastore in the centre of town. To hear him tell it, he was revolutionizing the business. Much to the chagrin of the traditional druggists around him, it was true. He sold drugs more cheaply than anyone else, calculating filling charges as a percentage of cost rather than as a flat fee. He kept his store open seven days a week. And he sold a wide

A MODERN-DAY
LONDON DRUGS STORE.

ABOVE: SAM BASS'S SECOND LONDON DRUGS OUTLET, LOCATED AT GRANVILLE AND GEORGIA IN DOWNTOWN VANCOUVER. BASS REVOLUTIONIZED THE DRUG STORE BUSINESS, CUTTING PRESCRIPTION PRICES AND STOCKING EVERYTHING FROM COSMETICS TO CAMERAS.

OPPOSITE: LONDON DRUGS' FOUNDER SAM BASS IN AN UNCHARACTERISTIC MOMENT OF REPOSE DURING A STORE OPENING IN THE 1960S.

range of merchandise not normally found in drugstores—from cosmetics to beachballs to cameras. The shelves displayed a little bit of everything, and the public—including Tong—loved it.

Bass sponsored the pioneering open-line radio show hosted by bad boy hotliner Pat Burns, who delighted in phoning up surprised company presidents and chewing them out in prime time for being unfair to their customers. Burns' consumer advocacy was just a little bit too strong to last on commercial radio, but in the meantime it was a theme with which Bass identified. He never tired of railing against "the drug cartel" that he claimed kept the price of prescription drugs artificially high, and he was happy to

portray himself as the defender of the little guy. Bass claimed his annual sales went from $50,000 to over $1 million in two years and in 1963 he did open an emporium at Granville and Georgia in the dead centre of Vancouver's downtown. It was 1,500 square feet. His next store was 8,000 square feet, then 12,000, then 17,000. By 1970 he was boasting "I own the Vancouver drug market," and nobody was scoffing. London Drugs had become one of those institutions BC people took to their hearts as being somehow uniquely in synch with their own maverick spirit, a landmark on the commercial landscape of BC, along with White Spot restaurants and Woodward's department store.

A London Drugs store in the 1960s. The signs in the window advertise just about everything except drugs.

ABOVE: HORDES OF SHOPPERS
WOULD CLOG THE AISLES AT
LONDON DRUGS STORE OPENINGS
IN THE 1960s.

OPPOSITE: "ATTENTION, SHOPPERS!"
MARK NUSSBAUM TAKES TO THE
AIRWAVES IN A LONDON DRUGS
STORE IN THE 1960s.

In 1968 Bass succumbed to an attractive offer from the Daylin Corporation of California and sold out. He remained president of the operation, with one of Daylin's men, Mark Nussbaum, sent to serve as watchdog. The company continued to be innovative, adding things like books, yard furniture and electronics to the stores' already eclectic inventory and enlarging the London Drugs chain to 10 locations in BC and Alberta. Things were going well in BC, but in the mid-1970s Daylin fell on hard times. Cash-starved and facing bankruptcy, it was forced to get rid of its ancillary holdings, including London Drugs. Another US-based store chain, Payless, held an option to buy London Drugs, but Payless was itself financially strapped and was unable to make good on its commitments. Another buyer would have to be found.

There are a number of stories of how Tong acquired the London Drugs chain. The most persistent one describes how, alerted to the Daylin/Payless situation, he instantly acted on his remarkable business instincts and—ignoring the warnings and advice of colleagues, lawyers and accountants—he concluded the transaction almost single handedly. In later years, even Tong began to believe this version of what happened.

It is very likely that his in-house advisors counselled against the move. After all, the rock on which the success of H.Y. Louie was founded was its expertise in the food industry. A drug store-cum-department store business would divert Tong far from his area of competence—and there lurked danger. Tong for his part seems to have felt a strong affinity with the London Drugs operation, founded as it was on Sam Bass's theory of delivering service and value, not unlike the code of conduct handed down by Hok Yat Louie. He liked the style of the company, and the place of affection it occupied in the hearts of Westerners.

The story told by other participants confirms Tong did follow his own instincts, but had good professional help in carrying the deal through. He also had that juicy I.O.U. to call in from the Royal Bank, which still wanted to make up its failure to support Tong in the Dominion stores acquisition.

Barry Dryvynsyde, with the law firm Bull, Housser & Tupper, says that representatives from Payless arrived in Vancouver in December 1976 intent on finding a buyer for the London Drugs stores. Dryvynsyde's law firm was asked to help with the search and contact potential candidates, which included Woodward's and Victor McLean, a prominent man in the food industry.

When they weren't interested Dryvynsyde and his colleagues decided to speak with Grant Hammond, the chartered accountant in charge of the H.Y. Louie account at the accounting firm of Touche Ross. With low expectations, Hammond went through the motion of informing his client of the business opportunity. He was surprised when Tong

showed interest—keen interest. In retrospect, Hammond thinks Tong must have heard rumours that Shoppers Drug Mart was closing in on the deal.

Tong asked Hammond to immediately obtain the Daylin files from Bull, Housser & Tupper, study them carefully and give him his opinion. Hammond felt the value of the properties alone made it attractive. But the performance figures were impressive, too. Some London Drugs units were yielding $3,000 per square foot, excellent for the time. Average gross margin was 25 percent. Tong needed no further convincing. He wanted to start negotiations as soon as they could be arranged, fearing that Shoppers Drug Mart was in pursuit. He instructed Hammond to assemble all the

players in the Vancouver head office of the Royal Bank as soon as possible. Brandt was given the job of alerting the bank and persuading its officials to give up their weekend of golf to do some serious financial transactions.

The first meeting was held on a Saturday morning in the third week of December. The negotiations didn't go all that smoothly. Since Payless would be involved in the final financing formula, a transcript of H.Y. Louie's financial statement was requested, a demand which Tong flatly refused. H.Y. Louie was a private company; he had never revealed its financial status before and he was not about to do it now. He couldn't be budged.

In the end, the Royal Bank prepared a statement testifying to H.Y. Louie's solvency and its ability to engage in a transaction of this magnitude. By Sunday afternoon, negotiations reached the first critical point. According to Mark Nussbaum, Shoppers Drug Mart was by this time openly bidding but dropped out when Tong raised the ante by $100,000. For $500,000 Tong obtained an option on the London Drugs properties. By this time he had already made up his mind that he wanted to buy the company but he wanted to eliminate all doubts. The option allowed him to fend off other interested parties while giving him the time to proceed a bit more slowly—but not much. For its own reasons, Daylin had to complete the transaction by year's end.

Racing the calendar, Tong met Ted Horsey, a Bull Housser lawyer, in Los Angeles two days later. They went to the Daylin offices where they delved as deeply as possible into the accounts in the short time they had at their disposal. Satisfied by what he found, Tong made an offer of $9 million. Daylin accepted it a few days before Christmas and Tong became owner of the London Drugs chain. It was the single most lucrative achievement of his career.

When all the documents were signed, the two men prepared to return to Vancouver, each going his separate way. Horsey returned to his hotel, packed his bags and taxied to the airport. He had a first-class ticket and was ready to board the plane when he spotted Tong entering economy. Horsey cancelled his flight. Here was his client, scant hours after signing a commitment for $9 million, choosing to fly economy class. He had an uneasy feeling that Tong would frown on the sight of his lawyer travelling first class.

Paul Trussell and his wife joined Tong and Geraldine for dinner at the Shaughnessy Golf and Country Club that evening. "During dinner, Tong casually mentioned that he had purchased London Drugs that day," said Trussell. "He was quite amused at the distress it had caused his accountants. Then he

went back to his study of the dessert menu. Geraldine seemed quite pleased with his decision, although I remember her saying she hoped he knew what he was doing."

As was his practice, Tong kept the company's best managers to help run the business and smooth the transition; in this case, Stan Glazier, who had taken over as CEO when Sam Bass resigned some months earlier. Glazier held the post until he got into a conflict with Tong about two years later and they parted ways. Mark Nussbaum then took over as the senior manager under Tong. Nussbaum was a graduate of the

"California" school of marketing. He had seen the advent of volume retail centres down there and Tong credited him with many of the innovations in product and marketing introduced by London Drugs, though his brash manner was at odds with Tong's style.

Other key personnel were Lennie Marks and Norm Hoff, both long-term executives with London Drugs and good friends of Tong. Hoff was a financial wizard, an accountant who looked after the financial aspects of the organization for over 20 years before he retired. Lennie Marks ran the pharmacy division and general merchandising of the company up until the late 1990s. He was described by one of his colleagues as "a very shrewd general merchandiser, a very good buyer, and very competent pharmacist." He helped move the pharmaceutical division of the company from being simply price-driven to a more service-oriented approach. The management team gained an important new member in November 1982 when Wynne Powell was recruited to deal with problems in the company's technical area. In the 1970s the chain had added consumer electronics and small appliances to its well-established camera section, but the department wasn't making money. Within eight months Powell turned it around, expanding one-hour photo processing service to all stores and moving into the new field of personal computing, positioning the company to become one of Canada's leading computer retailers by the 1990s. As Powell's professional accounting discipline, marketing street smarts and administrative abilities were observed by Nussbaum and Tong, he was given responsibility for merchandise administration and company marketing activities. In 1984 Tong asked him to join the executive committee and after Nussbaum left he took over as vice-president and senior manager under Tong, positions he held through the company's period of greatest growth until he was made company president and COO after Tong's death. As the century neared its end, the *Chain Drug Review* estimated London Drugs'

1.2 million square feet of selling space was generating in the neighbourhood of $1 billion in sales.

Even with a success story this big, Tong remained careful in his business dealings. He was a gambler, but a cautious one who was principally motivated by his vision of the future. Buying London Drugs was the most extreme example of his calculated foolhardiness—and he hit the jackpot.

In following years Tong would have many opportunities to invest in what appeared to be lucrative projects and programs. More often than not he avoided them, usually, as time would prove, to his advantage.

Tong never considered going public with his companies, giving his reasons quite candidly: "If you are a public company you are no longer your own boss. You have to issue annual reports and deal with difficult shareholders. As a private company we take our chances. Either we enjoy success or we suffer, but we answer to no one. I like it that way."

As chairman, president and chief executive officer of both H.Y. Louie and London Drugs, he divided his time between the two companies, following an inflexible routine. His day began when he rose, ate breakfast and headed for the YMCA. By 7 a.m. he was working out or running a park trail and by 8:30 a.m. he was behind his desk at H.Y. Louie where he spent the morning dealing with the affairs of that company. With time out for a Spartan lunch, he would make his way out to Horseshoe Place in Richmond where he settled himself behind another impressive desk for an afternoon of London Drugs business. By 6:30 or 7 p.m., he was home for the evening, or for a brief recess before he headed out to a charity function, or a committee meeting called by one of the many causes he had become involved in.

Tong had always been active in charities. As his businesses expanded and became more successful, he expanded his community participation. He supported a number of corporate and personal charities as well as cultural, medical and athletic causes, but he did it almost secretly. He didn't seek recognition for the work he did with Saint Paul's Hospital Foundation, the Pacific Otolaryngology Foundation, the United Way, the YMCA, the Vancouver Symphony Society, or any of the many other organizations he became involved with. He simply wasn't interested in personal kudos.

His philosophy, based in Confucian thought, was simple and he took no credit for it. "My dad made it clear to all of us," he said, "if the community gives to you or helps your business to become a success, then you must give back to the community. It is your duty and you should accept it willingly."

Linda Dickson worked as the director of the Saint Paul's Hospital Foundation for years and, in that time, had many opportunities to watch Tong at work. Saint Paul's was one of the first major charities he became involved with, and it was always one of his favourites.

"He was a philanthropist for all the right reasons," said Dickson. "No ulterior motives, no searching for credit or aggrandizement. He threw himself into any and every cause because a need was there and it had to be dealt with."

She met him for the first time during the campaign to fund Chinatown's Dr. Sun Yat-Sen Classical Chinese Gardens. He was deeply involved in the project and she was impressed with his no-nonsense approach to getting the job done. "He had no time for groundless chatter or pie-in-the-sky suggestions," she said. "There had to be a plan and it had to be practical and achievable, and it had to be executed efficiently and quickly."

He was so successful with the Sun Yat-Sen Gardens campaign that Dickson and others set about persuading him to become the chairman of a $6-million capital funding campaign for Saint Paul's Hospital.

"It took him a while to accept," said Dickson. "He wasn't interested in an honorary appointment. There was work involved, and he wouldn't have it any other way. When he accepted, things began to happen."

Tong immediately began strong-arming business friends and corporations for both money and active participation in the campaign.

"It was his version of putting your money where your mouth is," said Dickson. "Instead he asked them to put their energy and influence where their money was; a cheque plus personal participation. It worked wonderfully well. We were amazed at how many influential people this man knew, and how willingly they answered the call. Their response could only have been out of respect and liking for him."

From then on, Tong went on to captain several other campaigns for Saint Paul's. His influence on the foundation's annual fundraising program was profound. "The yearly fundraising breakfasts were crowded," said Dickson. "Everyone who was anyone was there—or had an ironclad excuse not to be.

"He combined the attack and precision of a first-class executive with a remarkable warmth of heart," she said. "In spite of his crowded business agenda, he would visit the foundation headquarters at Saint Paul's several times a week, usually after his YMCA workouts. He was always cheerful and encouraging, but you knew he was really there to find out how the donations were coming in—and who had to be prodded a little.

"I was a dog owner and he had two dogs, a boxer and a pointer. We would compare notes, and he would supply me with dog food samples picked up at IGA. At Christmas he brought little gifts for the foundation staff. Naturally we loved him dearly and would have done anything for him."

As Tong's companies grew he feared he was losing touch with his staff, and it was then he sought outside help. The solution he arrived at was to instill a feeling of family in his large organization by putting a face on

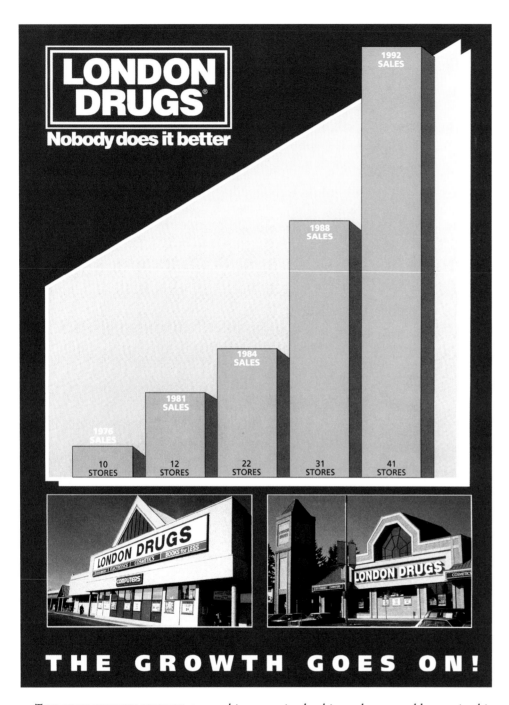

LONDON DRUGS®
Nobody does it better

1992 SALES

1988 SALES

1984 SALES

1981 SALES

1876 SALES

| 10 STORES | 12 STORES | 22 STORES | 31 STORES | 41 STORES |

THE GROWTH GOES ON!

THIS CHART FROM THE COMPANY MAGAZINE, LONDON BRIDGE, ILLUSTRATES THE PHENOMENAL GROWTH OF THE LONDON DRUGS CHAIN AFTER TONG BOUGHT IT IN 1976.

Some employee programs enjoyed success well beyond company walls.

An example of this was his sponsorship of the IGA basketball team that took on all comers one season, going on to win the Canadian Basketball Trophy—a remarkable undertaking for an upstart western team. The achievement made sports history, to the extent that, in April 1997, the team was admitted into the BC Sports Hall of Fame. Tong was asked to say a few words on that occasion, and shared some recollections:

"Some people will say I backed the IGA basketball team for the publicity and advertising," he said. "That is not entirely true. I enjoy sports immensely, and I welcomed the opportunity to support potential winners. They were winners. The advertising factor was questionable anyway. Irwin Swangard was sports editor of the *Vancouver Sun* at that time. He's a legend now that he is no longer with us, but he was also hard-nosed. He refused to use 'IGA' in any of his stories. He called the team 'the Grocers,' which meant that Safeway and SuperValu received as much credit for a winning team as IGA did. I still think they should have shared in the cost of the uniforms."

The winning team not only earned trophies, it gave IGA employees a reason to celebrate and boosted their company pride. Within both IGA and London Drugs, employees became self-starters in building and maintaining company morale. With Tong's blessing and some funding, choirs and instrumental groups formed. They practised voluntarily in their own time, and not only for the entertainment of their fellow employees at company functions and trade conventions; they went out into the community as well.

his companies that his employees would recognize: his own. Smiling, affable, pipe in place, but very much in command. His ability to project warmth and friendliness came naturally, and he learned to use that inborn tendency for his personnel-relations agenda.

CHAPTER 14

A Seat at the Table

In July 1979, Earl McLaughlin, president of the Royal Bank of Canada, phoned Tong from Montreal and invited him to become a member of the bank's board of directors. It was an honour and an opportunity most chief executive officers in Canada would have accepted immediately. Tong's reaction to the phone call was casual. He thanked McLaughlin politely, promised him he would think it over, and agreed to give him a decision in a day or two.

"If I thought it was some kind of condescending tokenism I would have turned them down right away," said Tong. "After all I was the first Chinese Canadian to receive an invitation like that."

There were many good reasons for the bank's choosing Tong. As president of H.Y. Louie and chairman of London Drugs, both large and thriving businesses, Tong had more than established his credentials on the BC business scene. He was one of the bank's largest BC customers and he also met the requirement that a director must hold more than 2,500 of the bank's shares. If his ethnicity entered into the decision, it might have been for the very legitimate consideration that he was an influential force in a

Chinese community that was now rebounding and becoming economically more powerful each year.

Five days after McLaughlin's phone call, Tong accepted the invitation. Newspapers and financial

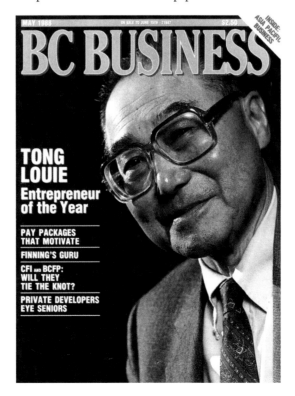

NOT EVEN THE PUBLICITY-SHY TONG COULD ESCAPE THE COVER OF *BC BUSINESS MAGAZINE* WHEN HE WAS NAMED BC'S ENTREPRENEUR OF THE YEAR FOR THE FIRST TIME IN 1988. HE WOULD RECEIVE THE HONOUR AGAIN SEVERAL YEARS LATER.

journals headlined the appointment, arousing a curiosity in Canada's business community to learn more about this man who had broken into the nation's inner banking circle. At the time, a Vancouver banker observed that it was a very unusual move for the Royal Bank. "This is the first director appointment to take place outside of the old boys' network," he said, "and a Chinese Canadian at that. I doubt if anything like this will happen again soon."

Tong was caught full face in the glare of publicity. He was the first member of a Canadian minority to crack the financial major leagues, a fiduciary Jackie Robinson. Say what you want about your first doctors and first professors, you know your community has arrived when one of its leaders is asked to be a director of the country's largest bank. Tong's days of operating in comfortable obscurity were over.

Other forms of recognition began to come his way. Family and friends who either had taken his activities for granted or were largely unaware of his work were now motivated to pay him more attention. Later he admitted that he was both surprised and bothered by this activity.

"People were finding ways to honour him for his success and it shocked him," said Helen Wong. "He had never taken time to consider that he might have achieved success. I think he was embarrassed. He didn't think he deserved this kind of attention and, to his credit, I don't think it spoiled him in any way. He decided to get used to it, tolerate it perhaps."

In the summer of 1979 friends in the food industry organized a party for Tong and Geraldine. Ostensibly, the event was to celebrate the couple's 38th anniversary but it conveniently coincided with what would, by normal standards, have been Tong's retirement year. William Boland of Somerville Belkin Industries hosted the event, which was attended by top executives of major retail and wholesale food industries from BC and other parts of Canada. Some were retired

but willingly accepted the invitation. John Baird of Kelly Douglas, Tom Farrell of Woodward's and Alex Hart, the senior vice-president of Canadian National Railways, were among the many people who showed up. Ironically, a number of the guests represented companies that had gone out of their way in the past to obstruct, if not eliminate, H.Y. Louie from competition. That night, they honoured Tong as a worthy competitor and an outstanding builder of their industry.

A long poem relating the story of Tong's climb to success was read and Geraldine was presented with a bouquet in recognition of the support she gave her husband throughout their long marriage. Tong responded to these gestures in a somewhat bemused fashion, wondering at the elaborate nature of the occasion. It was apparent, as he recalled highlights of the 50 years he spent in the industry, that all that time—when measured by the day-to-day, humdrum attention to business—did not seem to him to be worthy of this kind of attention. He promised the assembly that he would try to improve on his performance in the 50 years to come. There was no mention of retirement.

Tong faced each day as though he did have another 50 years of life ahead of him. His energy remained undiminished, as did his attention to his businesses now adapting to a dramatically changing environment.

The province had emerged from the '70s on the crest of an economic boom. Hok Yat Louie, urging his tired horse up a lonely road at the turn of the century, would have been amazed at the Vancouver skyline reaching for the clouds in the late '70s. Hastings Sawmill, where he had laboured in the early years, was long gone, replaced by wharves and warehouses that were themselves making way for first-class hotels, exotic restaurants and marinas catering to the yachts of millionaires. Seabuses shuttled tirelessly across Burrard Inlet to the North Shore, transporting those commuters not driving over the Lions Gate Bridge and the Second Narrows Bridge.

Granville Island had been transformed from an industrial eyesore into a colourful farmers' market enhanced with marinas, restaurants, galleries and office buildings. Adjacent to it, along False Creek, a dozen smoke-belching sawmills had been replaced with fashionable townhouses standing next to attractive affordable housing.

In 1971 Chinatown was named a historic site along with Gastown, Vancouver's first commercial centre. Federal immigration laws had eased, opening the door to newcomers from around the world. New ethnic neighbourhoods took shape in areas surrounding Fraser Street, Richmond and elsewhere. A number of people from Hong Kong, realizing that it was just a matter of time before Mainland China exercised its right to take over the territory, emigrated to Canada at this time. Real estate records reveal that as early as 1978 Hong Kong interests owned as much as half of Vancouver's most-valued office spaces and apartment complexes. Even in 1982, when a recession hit the country—resulting in a severe rise in unemployment and skyrocketing real estate prices—the new wave of immigration continued. In BC, the government of the day lowered the barriers to foreign investment, resulting in a surge of foreign capital, the majority of it from Asia. The Hong Kong Bank opened its doors in Vancouver and was doing a brisk business. In 1984, when Britain declared that Hong Kong would revert to China in 1997, the focus on Vancouver real estate intensified even further. From a low of 15,000 in 1951, British Columbia's Chinese-Canadian population climbed to an estimated 300,000 at the end of the century. As Tong noted in a 1997 television interview, the new Chinese immigrants received a very different welcome than the Chinese who came in the 1800s.

"Comparing the situation of Chinese arriving in Canada today with the Chinese of my father's day is like comparing apples and oranges," he said. "My father led a hard, marginal existence, hoping to find something better in Canada. He was almost penniless." The Chinese of today arrive with more than adequate financial resources, with business and professional skills, and often with a command of English. My father and every other Chinese immigrant in his day was the subject of powerful and persistent discrimination.

"The Chinese arriving here today are welcomed by governments and the business community. They enjoy the full range of Canadian rights, can practise any profession they choose, live anywhere they want, and take advantage of every educational opportunity. Times are much better than when I was a boy. Then my father had to contend with white competition that could be described as ruthless; now it has been replaced by the kind of competition to be expected in any marketplace—tough but typical. When I was young, no Chinese would think of trying to join the Vancouver Board of Trade. Today my son, Brandt, is chairman of the Vancouver Board of Trade.

"Times change. The past is history. It would be a mistake to forget the past entirely, but I think it is much more constructive to direct our energies to improving the future than dwelling on the past."

Although Tong could easily have afforded to speculate in Vancouver's real estate boom, he held back. His firm policy was to invest in property solely for the purpose of his own businesses, searching for and finding prime locations for future stores and warehouses. Even when Brandt, who had become the vice-president of H.Y. Louie in 1977, became temporarily sold on the opportunities of the booming real estate market, he couldn't persuade his father to join in the money rush.

"One of his greatest strengths was his ability to see and anticipate problems down the road," said Brandt. "When I thought we should be moving in a certain direction he warned me against it. He said that now was a better time to strengthen the balance sheet.

THIS PAGE: TODAY'S SOPHISTICATED MARKETPLACE IGA STORES HAVE COME A LONG WAY FROM THEIR HUMBLE BEGINNINGS, BUT THEY STILL EMPHASIZE THE FRESH PRODUCE THAT HAS ALWAYS BEEN THE HALLMARK OF H.Y. LOUIE STORES.

OPPOSITE: AFTER A 15-YEAR APPRENTICESHIP THAT INCLUDED EVERYTHING FROM WORKING AS A CLERK IN AN IGA STORE TO MERCHANDISING MANAGER OF H.Y. LOUIE, BRANDT LOUIE BECAME PRESIDENT OF THE FAMILY FIRM IN 1987.

He said that inflation would come full circle and tough times would occur. Of course he was right."

In the early 1980s the economy went into recession and the real estate market crashed, ruining many who had succumbed to its appeal.

Brandt was very involved in the family businesses and he helped his father make them ride with the times, catering to new tastes and product preferences. The inventories of H.Y. Louie and London Drugs took on a new look dictated not only by tastes of a multicultural population but also by rapidly advancing technology. The One-Hour Photo Labs, introduced in 1981 and later expanded to all stores by Wynne Powell, soon became as much a company trademark as its discount prescriptions. The full-service computer departments added by Powell in 1983, before most people even knew what a floppy disk was, had positioned the company at the forefront of the hottest consumer trend of the decade. Even during the recession it was able to open new complexes at the rate of one or two a year, each providing thousands of square feet of diverse merchandise as well as the prescription services that justified its name. By 1989 the company owned 34 stores in British Columbia and Alberta.

A couple of years earlier, Brandt had become the president of H.Y. Louie after completing a 15-year apprenticeship that included positions as IGA clerk, buyer and merchandising director, as well as a 10-year term as vice-president. He says his father never coerced him into joining the family business. "He gave me advice as to careers, but he left the decision up to me, just as he did with my brother, Kurt. I think I followed my father into the business more by osmosis than anything. I grew up surrounded by his activities and it got into my blood."

As he became involved in the family business he had days when he felt fortunate to be Tong Louie's son and days when he didn't. He quotes the old adage, "It's hard to grow in the shadow of a mountain."

"I believe it will always be a more difficult situation between a father and a son in the workplace," Brandt says. "But I'm one of the lucky ones. I've survived and I'm stronger for it. But then, I've learned from one of the best."

By the time he became president the food industry had changed. The superstores like Costco, the Real Canadian Superstore and Save-On-Foods arrived in Vancouver in the early 1980s, dazzling customers with their huge floor space and endless selection of products. This was a new ball game in which H.Y. Louie chose not to play. The Louies agreed with the directors of IGA Canada to maintain IGA stores at an intermediate size with all shelves and departments conveniently available to the average shopper.

In Tong's estimation, the concept of the superstore would overwhelm the shopper. In 1990 when the Western Canada Food Industry presented him with an Astra award in recognition, not only of his long years in the industry, but for his continuing performance in the business, he gave his semi-facetious opinion on the subject of superstores.

"Shopping in one of the megastores calls for a degree of stamina and endurance never required in the

lazy days of the local grocery store," he said. "Today a customer walks 50 yards east to find a pound of tea, continues 75 yards north to search for a can of cream, then 60 yards west to locate the sugar. It's a great cardiac workout.

"I have seen pensioners standing at the checkout counters, out of breath and perspiring from trotting up and down the food aisles. It has reached a point where store managers are going to have to install showers."

In a more serious vein he wondered, "just how big can megastores get before they lose whatever advantages they promote, before big ceases to be better?"

Brandt Louie's vision for H.Y. Louie and its IGA affiliates as mid-sized outlets with strong neighbourhood connections dovetails with that of his father.

"There will always be a place for neighbourhood-based entrepreneurs, who are involved in their communities, who have found their niche serving their customers the way they want and need to be served," Brandt says. "When you're an independent grocer, it's almost impossible to compete head to head with the big guys operating discount supermarkets. Instead you must compete on value, meaning a combination of price competitiveness and quality. It also includes things like differentiating the look of your store and merchandising products geared directly to your customers' desires, and being an integral part of the community you serve."

In support of this outlook IGA is renovating many BC stores in keeping with a country marketplace theme, featuring photographic wall-murals with scenes from local history and promoting a "Hometown Proud" campaign to support community groups. Some stores donate a percentage of each purchase toward new computers for local schools. It all comes back to Brandt's belief that "the ability to understand who your customers are and to have the willingness to serve those customers are what's going to make or break any company." It is a belief he in turn traces back to his grandfather, whose letters urging his heirs to "be earnest, fair and loyal in dealing with customers" are still proudly displayed on the walls of the company's office.

CHAPTER 15

Laurels and Sorrows

As promised, Tong played an active role when he joined the board of the Royal Bank. He served on key committees and gave a good account of himself for five years. But he was 65 when he joined and the bank had a policy of retiring directors at age 70, so in 1984 he was forced to resign. Tong handled his departure from the Royal with the usual light touch, although his reference to old age reflected a more than casual resistance to the aging process.

"I am standing before you tonight to perform my swan song," he said. "A swan song, as I understand it, is what a very old and shaky bird does in the way of saying farewell.

"I can assure you that the suggestion that I might be an old bird causes my feathers to ruffle . . . this occasion marks my departure into forced senility, based on the bank's official premise that, when a director reaches the age of 70, suddenly and mysteriously his lights go out. Tonight the bank is throwing the switch in a most auspicious manner, and I will go out of here trying to find my way with a candle."

While Tong's aging might have prevented him from continuing as an active member of the Royal

Bank's board of directors, it didn't stop him from sitting on a spate of other boards and committees, including those of many charities. As he got older his reputation began overtaking him and more and more honours came his way. On September 14, 1985, Tong became the first Canadian to receive the Variety Club's Gold Heart Award, joining such luminaries as Nancy Reagan and Johnny Carson. The presentation was made at a banquet emceed by Monty Hall and attended by Joseph Sinay, the Variety Club's president, along with a stellar lineup of prominent Vancouver people. Hall enthused about the work Tong had done on behalf of the British Columbia's Children's Hospital Fund. Tong's response was heartfelt but characteristically brief. In essence he wondered why he should be rewarded for doing something that needed to be done; something he enjoyed and took pride in doing.

"I've always had food and shelter," he said. "There are others who don't and I'm in a position to help them. It's not a subject for debate. If you can help someone you should." It was a theme he would find himself repeating often in the next few years.

GOVERNOR GENERAL JEANNE
SAUVÉ ADMITS TONG TO THE
ORDER OF CANADA IN OCTOBER
1989.

TONG CELEBRATES HIS ELEVATION
TO KNIGHT OF THE GOLDEN
PENCIL WITH SENATOR
RAY PERRAULT IN 1989.

By this time, Vancouver was well established as a thriving, cosmopolitan city. BC Place Stadium, the first covered structure of its kind in Canada, opened its turnstiles to the public in 1983. Under the gleaming white dome the BC Lions football team struggled with mixed success. Premier Bill Bennett revealed an ambitious dream that would attract international attention to the city and the province while, he hoped, earning kudos for his Social Credit government. His proposal was to mark Vancouver's centennial in 1986 by making it the site of a world exposition based on the theme of transportation and communications. The idea caught on after some resistance from the more cautious representatives of the civic and business community who, like Mayor Gerry McGeer's detractors during the

jubilee celebrations of 1936, felt the money would be better spent fighting effects of the ongoing recession. Expo 86 received an official launch when Queen Elizabeth appeared before a packed audience in BC Place Stadium.

The north side of False Creek was designated the Expo site. Once the home of sawmills, foundries and the wartime shipyards, the entire Creek underwent a massive facelift, beginning with a dredging operation to remove the industrial sludge of a century, followed by the shoring up of the crumbling shoreline. Soon a wonderland of pavilions, stages, rides, outdoor art and ethnic restaurants arose along the water, with the flags of many nations flying above it. The transportation theme was underlined by a new rapid transit system linking Vancouver with New Westminster and a new highway following the course of the Coquihalla River to the interior of the province, reducing car travel by two hours.

Tong was keenly interested in this project, not only because an influx of visitors would be good for business, but because it raised the city to a new level of international prestige. He felt satisfaction in the fact that Expo's glittering perimeter was a few short blocks from his place of birth. The soaring geodesic dome of Science World occupied a site where he had hunted for bullheads as a boy.

His enthusiasm was rudely interrupted in the midst of Expo euphoria, however. On May 1, 1986, the day the gates to Expo 86 opened to the public, Geraldine entered Saint Paul's Hospital and underwent bypass surgery.

Geraldine's long-time friends say she had been frail as a girl and never enjoyed robust health as an adult. While she never had to face the kind of labour Tong's mother endured, her life as the wife of an over-achieving husband and mother of three children had not been easy. Although the surgery was successful, she never fully regained her health.

Tong's own bout of illness 12 years earlier had made him more health conscious but even though he was careful to eat well and exercise regularly, the effects of his diabetes still had a major impact. George Langley, one of his golfing partners, got used to watching out for him.

"He was insulin-dependent," said Langley. "Hypoglycemia [low blood sugar] goes with the disease, and Tong would forget to take precautions. I sometimes think he was in perpetual denial, refusing to accept the fact that he was a diabetic. In the course of the game he would become confused both in speech and action. We would march him off to the clubhouse where a sandwich and a glass of orange juice usually returned him to normal. Then it was back to golf."

Once, while making an acceptance speech for one of the honours he received, he went into hypoglycemic shock. The most serious incident, however, took place in September 1986, just a few months after Geraldine's surgery.

While driving on a rainy night, having neglected to follow his diet that day, Tong went into shock. The accident that followed might have been fatal had it not been for the activation of an air bag. As it was, he suffered broken ribs and severe bruising. Worse, from his point of view, was his doctor's decision that he would have to stop driving. Tong liked cars and this restriction was difficult to accept. He hired a driver and in spite of being in obvious pain, he was soon back in full stride.

He credited Geraldine with saving his life. She had taken care of the details for delivery of his latest car and unknown to him, she had ordered air bags—considered an extra at that time.

"I don't know what surprised me more," said Tong, "the vague memory of the car going out of control, or the air bag popping out of nowhere to punch me in the chest."

In May 1988, Tong was chosen British Columbia's Entrepreneur of the Year, a joint award of Montreal Trust and *BC Business* magazine. The same year, the YMCA of Greater Vancouver named him Outstanding Community Volunteer Leader. He was cited for his years of work on behalf of the YMCA, including several years at board level.

On October 17, 1989, Geraldine accompanied Tong to Ottawa to see him receive the Order of Canada, the nation's highest civilian award. It was a poignant moment for both of them, and a powerful testament to the distance Chinese-Canadian citizens had travelled since the time when Hok Yat first arrived in Canada.

A month later it was time for another bouquet, this time the Food Industry Association of Canada's

OPPOSITE: DURING THE 49 YEARS OF THEIR MARRIAGE GERALDINE WAS TONG'S CLOSEST FRIEND AND CONFIDANT.

Knights of the Golden Pencil Award, the highest honour conferred by that organization.

The introduction testified to Tong's "impressive achievements as a gifted and successful business-man ... honours have come late for Tong Louie, but they are no less deserved. If one more honour were to be bestowed, it should be for his inherent modesty and genuine humanity."

In response, Tong suggested that the only reason he had been selected for the award was because he was the oldest member of the Food Industry Association still holding onto a job.

"My athletic prowess might have been a factor in choosing me," he said, "although I doubt it. The rumour that I am competing in the next Hawaiian ironman contest is completely unfounded. Four days a week I jog a few miles. Then I go to Hawaii to collapse.

"Someone tried to explain to me that I was selected because I am some kind of role model for the food industry. Ladies and gentlemen, if the Food and Drug Act had been in effect in 1930 when I started I would be in a Western jail somewhere."

He went on to relate how he had concocted his own products: jelly powders, prunes moistened with surplus molasses, mustard laced with flour, vinegar diluted with water.

"No one was poisoned," he said. "The customer was satisfied with the product, and H.Y. Louie earned a few pennies per item. One way or another most of us made it through very tough times with a little resourcefulness and some help from our friends. Now we can remember and laugh at ourselves a bit."

In early July 1990, while driving in the city, Geraldine suffered a stroke, crashed her car and was rushed to hospital. Whether the after-effects of heart surgery contributed to the attack is not clear. She never recovered and passed away at the age of 71 on July 30, 1990.

Tong was shattered.

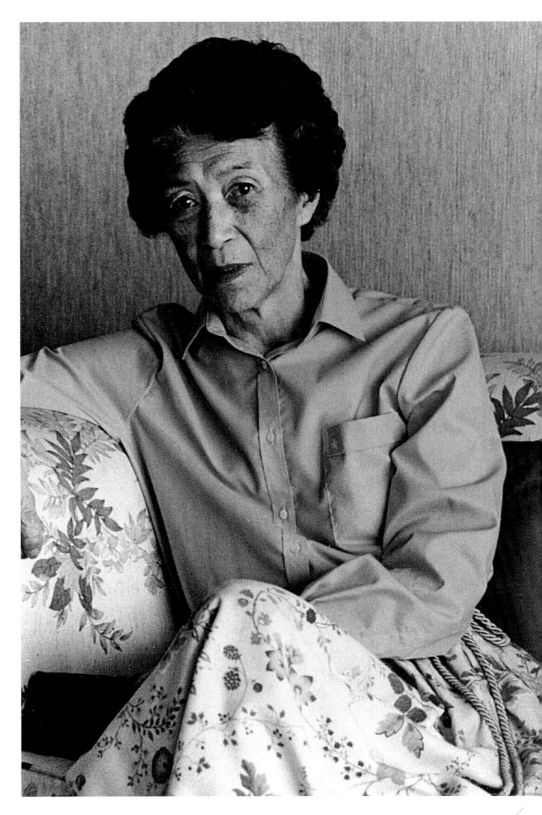

Like many husbands, he had taken for granted the contributions made by his spouse. Not until her death did he realize just how much he relied on her. "She never complained of bad health," said Helen Wong, who had numerous conversations with Geraldine over the years. "But on one occasion, commenting on what Tong would do if she were no longer there for him she said, 'I think Tong will miss me when I die. He will have no one to scold.'"

Now she was gone and he missed her desperately.

For over 40 years, Geraldine, the mysterious uptown girl whose confidence in Western circles had so beguiled him as a youth, had been Tong's closest friend and most loyal champion. She took care of his everyday needs, raised their children, promoted his intellectual growth and served as his worthy partner as together they led their people onto the main stage of Canadian society.

Family friends and Tong's business associates were shocked and saddened by her unexpected death. John Lowe was one of the many people who saw how much Geraldine's death hurt Tong.

"He was not good at expressing his personal feelings," said Lowe, "but his deep grief was evident and he didn't quite know how to cope with it. He named London Drugs' new head office after her as a way to perpetuate her name."

"She accompanied Tong on many dealer trips in North America and overseas," said Ed Hellinger, "and on no occasion was she in any way overbearing. She never played the part of the president's wife. She was just one of us, with no expectation of special attention or treatment. She made a point of remaining detached from Tong's business, but provided him at all times with moral support and a strong home base."

Geraldine was the mediator between Tong and his daughter when, well along in her university studies, Anndraya declared she wanted to do what many of her friends had done and move out on her own.

"Dad simply couldn't understand why I would want to do that," she said. "I describe him as having a Chinese heart and a Western attitude. It was traditionally Chinese for family members to live at home until they married but that's not the way it was in my environment."

Tong invited her to live at home as long as she wanted, and to pay room and board if that would make her feel more independent. She left home in 1981 at the age of 23. She then further asserted her independence by changing her name from Andrea Louie to Anndraya Luui.

Anndraya described her mother as "meticulous to a driven degree."

"She was a quiet but determined perfectionist, and like many conscientious parents she had chosen a career for me. It was to be either medicine or law. Mother had come close to becoming a doctor." Anndraya graduated with an arts degree.

"My mother made many of my father's decisions outside of his businesses," she said. "For instance, she led him into an appreciation of culture, although I don't think she ever converted him completely to symphony or ballet. His main pleasure was in musicals: *The King and I, My Fair Lady, Oklahoma!* and that sort of thing."

Ed Hellinger also noticed that, "she put him in touch with the arts, which he enjoyed but never embraced except as a friendly, supportive and eminently generous patron."

Of necessity Tong's lifestyle changed. Banned from driving, he now had to rely on a chauffeur. Without Geraldine he had to rely on a housekeeper to prepare his meals and keep the Southlands home in order. Loneliness was an experience he had never prepared for, and although his grief diminished with time, he never stopped mourning her. His friends were unanimous in observing that Geraldine's passing was the most traumatic thing he ever endured.

CHAPTER 16

A Brother Remembered

Many who were close to Tong, but who perhaps didn't know him as well as they thought, assumed and hoped that in the months following Geraldine's death he would finally slow down. They were disappointed. He threw himself into his physical regimen with undiminished vigour and immersed himself in his business routine. His driver resigned himself to dropping off Tong at the YMCA or Stanley Park every day by 7 a.m. before taking him to his two head offices.

Although others now handled many of Tong's executive tasks and Brandt was firmly entrenched in command of H.Y. Louie, Tong insisted on keeping a full work schedule. He spent his mornings at Lake City and his afternoons at Horseshoe Place. In the evenings he watched sports on television or attended meetings or charitable events.

Tong was in his seventies when he was first asked to chair formal meetings, in particular those of the University of British Columbia's property committee. Not quite sure of the proper etiquette involved, he got hold of an abbreviated *Roberts Rules of Order*, and taught himself how it was properly done. Most of his extra curricular meetings related to charities he was involved with, not only administratively but also as a principal donor. Despite the fact that he gave away millions of dollars to these organizations, he rarely had cash in his pockets. During coffee breaks, he would search in embarrassment for a few coins and end up letting someone else pay. It was a curious anomaly for a man who was in every other way highly self-sufficient and well organized.

"There is no doubt that Dad suffered from 'Depression syndrome'," said Kurt. "He never quite recovered from the days when he had absolutely nothing and was obliged to shop for bargains. I remember, just a few years ago, he bought a winter coat at the Three Vets (an army surplus store in Vancouver) for $29. It was heavy as lead and hung on him like a tent. I asked him if he bought it by the pound. The whole family remembers the red and yellow tweed suit he bought at Chapman's for 60 percent off. The store should have given it away."

Another manifestation of the Depression syndrome showed up when Tong travelled abroad.

MAINTAINING A TRADITION THAT
SPANS THREE GENERATIONS,
BRANDT LOUIE IS THE FOURTH
MEMBER OF HIS FAMILY TO HEAD
H.Y. LOUIE CO. LIMITED.

OPPOSITE: MARKETPLACE IGA
STORES FEATURE WELL-STOCKED
DELIS.

"Almost every time he travelled he brought back merchandise that might, just might, catch on in the Canadian market," Kurt said. "I remember ladies' chains, belts, and other items from Hong Kong, turtle meat and kangaroo tail soup from Australia, and other exotic items from who knows where on the other side of the globe. Sometimes his judgment was good; sometimes it was not, and his experiment went the way of the discount shelf. I suspect he brought back new sales items to justify his travels. He didn't need to but his ingrained work ethic never left him, even when he was supposed to be on a travel holiday."

Once a week, Tong paid a morning visit to the Produce Terminal, a related Louie company on Malkin Avenue, where he shared a coffee, talked business and reminisced with president John Chin.

Chin had come a long way from his mom-and-pop store experience back in the early 1950s. After his Pay Low retail store failed, Tong hired him and dispatched him to Vernon to open a cash-and-carry outlet for the company.

"I couldn't believe I was doing this," Chin said. "Here I was trying to get over the shock of a failed business, with no education to speak of, with my self-confidence shaken, on the way to an Okanagan town to take care of all of the details of a cash-and-carry operation. Tong insisted that I do it, he wouldn't allow me to refuse."

Chin rose to the occasion and got the business started within the time frame Tong had specified. But when Tong asked him to stay in Vernon as manager of the new outlet he refused, citing responsibilities in Vancouver, and the unwillingness of his family to move.

"Tong wasn't happy," he recalls. "He could have turned his back on me but he didn't. He asked me to train someone else for the management job, and the man he gave me was a 53-year-old garage mechanic, Gordie Chan, with no experience in the food business whatever. I didn't say it to his face but I thought Tong

A number of years later Chin asked Tong why he had chosen a garage mechanic to manage a food outlet. "He took good care of my car," said Tong. "He was businesslike and organized. On top of that I knew he liked the outdoors. There's good hunting and fishing around Vernon, and it seemed to me Gordie would do a good job in those surroundings."

Chin became produce coordinator for H.Y. Louie, in spite of his insistence that he wasn't qualified for the job. When H.Y. Louie took over Terminal Fruit and Produce Company and renamed it Produce Terminal, Chin was seconded from H.Y. Louie to oversee the operation. In 1982, Brandt made him the company's president.

Now Tong regularly visited him, sipping coffee and discussing the latest feats and defeats of the athletes of the day. Occasionally he shared a few confidences with him—very few.

"Tong was an extremely private man," said Chin. "He kept his successes and troubles to himself. But when his wife died he couldn't keep that to himself. He suffered and it showed."

Despite the business responsibilities that often forced his family to take a back seat, Tong almost always acknowledged birthdays and other family anniversaries with a telephone call, a visit or a dinner. When Geraldine was alive she had kept contact with both sides of the family on a day-to-day basis. Tong simply didn't have that kind of time—although whenever he was in town and not tied down by business he was happy to be part of any family event Geraldine organized.

Now, without Geraldine to help him handle family matters, he had to find more time to do it himself. He made a heartfelt effort to get closer to his daughter, sons and grandchildren. In January 1997, he invited all available relatives to join him on a Mexican cruise. It was the last time that many family members were together with him.

TONG ON A RARE HOLIDAY IN PUERTO VALLARTA, FEBRUARY, 1997, WITH JOHN CHIN, MANAGER OF THE PRODUCE TERMINAL. TONG HIRED CHIN AFTER THE LATTER'S STORE HAD FAILED, AND KEPT PROMOTING HIM EVEN WHEN CHIN DOUBTED HIS OWN ABILITIES.

was really off course. I didn't know that he had a real talent for taking the true measure of people.

"He saw something in me I didn't know I had. The same with Gordie Chan. I took Chan up to Vernon, showed him the ropes, helped him with the inventory and hiring, and was back to Vancouver in a month. Gordie handled the business like a veteran."

As a grandfather he was attentive considering his busy schedule, taking his grandchildren on fishing trips, to the Olympics and to other events he thought they might enjoy.

Willis, Tong's second youngest brother, introduced him to salmon fishing in the late 1970s. Sixteen years separated them and, while Tong remained close to the entire family, Willis had always regarded him as somewhat out of reach and absorbed in business activities in which he had no part. Willis graduated from the University of British Columbia and chose a career in the insurance business.

Time closed the age gap. In June 1978, two years after the London Drugs takeover, Willis sensed a lull in his brother's relentless agenda, and suggested that Tong go on a fishing trip with him.

"We got into fish," recalls Willis, "and I had to coach him a little. Like any new fisherman his tendency was to

CHUCK CANDY, BRANDT LOUIE AND KARL VETTER IN THE UNPRETENTIOUS H.Y. LOUIE OFFICES IN BURNABY.

ALL IS WELL WITH THE WORLD:
TONG COMBINES TWO OF HIS
FAVOURITE MEANS OF RELAXING:
SMOKING HIS PIPE AND FISHING.

reel in furiously as soon as he had a salmon on the hook. I had to persuade him to let the fish run, and that wasn't in Tong's nature. His instinct was to get the job done as soon as possible, but he learned soon enough that you don't catch big salmon with that technique."

Salmon fishing became one of Tong's few methods of relaxation, and two or three times a year he went on fishing trips; later with grandchildren in the boat, teaching them as he had been taught by Willis. On some occasions he would join other friends and business associates fishing for tyee salmon in the Queen Charlottes where he landed several salmon well over 13 kilograms. Practical as ever, he would return to Vancouver with his big catch and drive straight to one

of the IGA stores to have his salmon cut and wrapped in manageable portions.

As with Geraldine's passing, Tong never quite got over the death of his brother Quan, who was killed in action with the RCAF in the closing months of the Second World War. Willis, who was 12 years old when Quan went to war, had also been struck by his older brother's death, and he took a special interest in his air force experiences.

In 1985, Willis travelled to England to learn more about Quan's last days. The airfield used by the Snowy Owl Squadron had reverted to farmland. The hangars and barracks were gone. Only the control tower remained, its paint fading, its interior filled with hay and farm implements. Willis described the visit as haunting. He found himself picturing the Halifax bombers deployed for takeoff, the air crews suited up for action, Quan among them, the only Chinese Canadian in the squadron, about to embark on his 28th and final sortie.

"We walked around the control tower," said Willis. "There were names scratched or written on all four walls, most of them faded or impossible to read. Quan's must have been there somewhere but I couldn't find it. So I wrote his name in. It belonged there."

Willis reported his experience to Tong, who decided immediately to pay his own visit to the airfield as soon as he could find the time. In 1987, he and Geraldine flew to England and made their way to Tholthorpe, where they experienced the same sadness and nostalgia as Willis.

"You saw the names on the walls," said Tong. "Then you could almost see the faces. All of them young, all of them gone. Quan was there."

It was rare to see Tong display emotion, but his eyes were misted, and he changed the topic quickly.

The details of Quan's death had always been sketchy and the visit to the derelict airfield moved Willis and Tong to learn more about his last days. Willis spent months tracking down information. Canadian and British air force records provided him with many details. The German military records were also remarkably informative.

It was known that Quan had died with most of his fellow crewmembers on January 16, 1945. The Halifax bomber's two air gunners had succeeded in bailing out before the plane crashed in flames. The focus was now on these two survivors. If either one

WAR BUDDIES: RCAF BOMBER PILOT **BILL WATSON** AND HIS BOMBARDIER, **FLYING OFFICER QUAN LOUIE.**

ON JANUARY 16, 1945, less than four months before Victory in Europe was declared on May 8, Flying Officer Quan Louie boarded a Halifax III A bomber with six of his crewmates and a pilot in training. Their mission was a nighttime raid over the German city of Magdeburg, an important target for the allies. Located on the Elbe River, it was the largest city in Saxony, had the second most important railroad junction in all of Germany, and was home to engineering works, aero-engine factories, an explosive factory and a large synthetic oil plant. Quan's crew set out with approximately 400 other Halifax bombers and Lancasters to destroy these structures. The importance of their targets and the scale of the attack were not the only things that would have made this particular sortie exciting for Quan. Thirty trips constituted a tour, after which an officer would be free to return home, and this was Quan's 28th mission.

Despite the crew's experience, gunner Doug Jacobi remembers they felt flustered. At the last minute they were asked to lead the formation in a plane other than the one they were used to and found themselves having to accommodate the trainee pilot. If this wasn't enough, the night was so dark they had to put on their landing lights to avoid mid-air collisions. The Halifax crossed the channel at low altitude, flying a mere 152 metres (500 feet) to 304 metres (1,000 feet) above the water, then quickly rising up to between 3,660 metres (12,000 feet) and 3,960 metres (13,000 feet) once it reached the mainland and enemy territory. Once they passed the Dutch coast they would begin dropping tin foil behind them to confuse enemy radar. As they neared

their target area, Quan would have taken up his usual position at the nose of the craft, lying on his belly on a narrow plank ahead of the navigator. As bomb aimer, or bombardier, his duty was to sight the Halifax's target and pull the trigger. It was a harrowing job. More than a couple of times in the past the plane had to dodge flak and once an enemy fighter followed them in their target area. As for the plane, in the past the crew's own Halifax had been forced down to 1,524 metres (5,000 feet) over enemy territory by icing and just a month earlier there had been hydraulic failure on the plane's takeoff wheels and bomb bay doors. Beyond this, the Halifax bombers were not known for their stealth, agility or speed, and by this point in the war thousands of RCAF airmen had been killed in action.

Quan's plane became separated from the other bombers and arrived three to four minutes late over a city already in flames. It was able to drop its load, but as it circled to return to England it was struck by anti-aircraft fire, caught fire and plummetted toward the ground.

For months the Louie family knew very little about what had happened to Quan. A couple of days after his plane disappeared a curt telegram arrived announcing that he was missing. A few days later, a letter arrived from Wing Commander W.G. Phelan, commanding officer of the Snowy Owl squadron, explaining that the crew had taken off from the airbase the evening of January 16 and had not been heard from since then.

"Your son had previously completed several successful sorties over enemy territory," wrote Phelan. "He was very popular throughout the

Squadron and particularly with the other members of his crew." He went on to add that his possessions were being packed up and forwarded to a central depository. "My hope that good news may be forthcoming to allay your anxiety is shared by the entire squadron and I wish to assure you that any information received will be immediately passed on to you."

In August, a few months after VE day, more information did arrive from an RCAF Casualty Officer who reported that Pilot Officer Doug Jacobi and Flight Sergeant Ted Lynch, two members of Quan's crew, had bailed from the plane, been taken as prisoners of war and eventually freed.

"Pilot Officer Jacobi... believes that the front escape hatch might have jammed and so prevented the other members from making their escape and that they went down with the aircraft," wrote the officer.

His letter ended with, "I again wish to assure you that when any additional information is received concerning your son, it will be forwarded to you. However, I am sure you will realize that owing to the chaotic conditions existing in Europe at the present time and the great number of enquiries confronting these enquiry services, some time may pass before more information is received."

It would be another four years before the family received any more news about Quan.

In January 1949, Quan's remains were located in the village of Bahrendorf, Germany, 19 kilometres south of Magdeburg. "Information was secured from a local resident that the aircraft had crashed about a mile east of the village. Your son and the four members of his crew all lost their lives and were buried in a single grave which was marked 'Hier ruhen 6 Kanadier-16.1.45'[Herein rest 6 Canadians]." His body was moved to the British Military Cemetery in Berlin. The wing commander promised that trees, shrubs and flowers would be planted, a permanent headstone erected at his burial site and that it would be cared for in perpetuity.

"I realize that this is an extremely distressing letter, and that there is no manner in which such news can be conveyed to you which would not add to your heartaches, and I am fully aware that nothing I say will lessen your great sorrow, but I would like to take this opportunity of expressing to you and the members of your family my deepest sympathy in the loss of your gallant son."

In total 17 bombers failed to return from the night's operation, including seven Canadian Halifaxes. Widespread fires and explosions hurled smoke into the air and caused a glow in the sky that was visible even from far away—evidence that the mission accomplished much of what it set out to do.

"This was our contribution to the Second World War," said Quan's younger brother Willis Louie. "It's just like my dad: he made out pretty good here, we made out pretty good here, so we decided to fight for Canada."

He repeated something Tong once said: "My brother Quan, he was born a Canadian. He fought as a Canadian. He died as a Canadian. You couldn't want anything more than that."

OPPOSITE: A HALIFAX BOMBER RETURNS FROM A MISSION.

QUAN AND HIS CREW MEMBERS STANDING BEFORE THEIR HALIFAX BOMBER. FROM LEFT TO RIGHT: NAVIGATOR KEN DOMINICK, DOUG JACOBI, ENGINEER AL PARKER, QUAN, DES PARTRIDGE, AN AIR GUNNER, AND PILOT BILL WATSON.

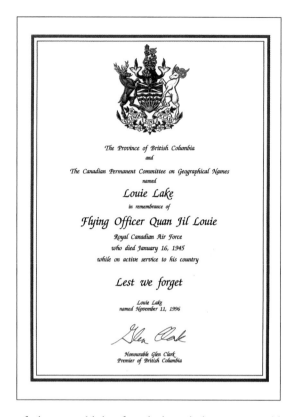

The Province of British Columbia
and

The Canadian Permanent Committee on Geographical Names
named

Louie Lake
in remembrance of

Flying Officer Quan Jil Louie

Royal Canadian Air Force
who died January 16, 1945
while on active service to his country

Lest we forget

Louie Lake
named November 11, 1996

Glen Clark

Honourable Glen Clark
Premier of British Columbia

ABOVE: IN NOVEMBER 1997, A LAKE
IN THE CAPILANO WATERSHED
NORTH OF VANCOUVER WAS NAMED
LOUIE LAKE IN MEMORY OF WAR
HERO QUAN LOUIE.

OPPOSITE: PREMIER
RITA JOHNSTON AWARDS TONG
THE ORDER OF BRITISH COLUMBIA
IN 1991.

PAGE 182: TONG CUTS THE RIBBON
AT THE OPENING OF THE DR. TONG
LOUIE LIVING LABORATORY IN
NOVEMBER 1997.

payload in the glare of searchlights all focussed on the solitary plane. Anti-aircraft guns went to work directing a concentrated barrage from which the bomber could not escape. Out of control and in flames it crashed near Behrendorf, taking Quan and four of his fellow crewmembers. Only the two gunners escaped.

Half a century after Quan died, Jacobi's visit with the Louie family brought closure to Quan's loss. The following year a tribute was paid to Quan on Remembrance Day 1996, when the BC Ministry of Environment, Lands and Parks bestowed his name upon a pristine lake a few kilometres north of Vancouver in the Capilano watershed, forever after to be known as Louie Lake. Tong took great satisfaction from this rare honour.

"It wasn't just his death," said Tong. "It was what he and other Chinese Canadians died for. It was for Canada, because he was a Canadian born and bred. But it was for Canadian Chinese as well. In 1947 we got the vote and all the rights and privileges denied to Chinese Canadians up until then."

Finally, on May 17, 1997, the Louie family presented a memorial plaque to Pacific Unit 280, Army, Navy and Air Force Veterans in Canada. It testified to the last flight of Quan Louie and his fellow airmen, and helped mark the 50th anniversary of Pacific Unit 280 as well as the 50th year of the granting of the vote to Chinese Canadians—a government act motivated largely by the voluntary enlistment, service and death of Chinese Canadians in the Second World War.

Willis Louie presented the plaque in a moving ceremony at the Chinese Canadian Culture Centre. Permanently on display, it includes a photograph of Quan, together with his service medals, a photograph of the Halifax bomber in which he served, and the names of all the crewmembers in that final flight in January 1945.

Quan Louie is buried in the British Military Cemetery in Berlin.

of them could be found the whole story would unfold.

The gunners had parachuted into enemy territory where they became prisoners of war. After the war they returned to civilian life. The attempt to search for one gunner, Ted Lynch, ended when they found out he had died, but the search for the other one, Doug Jacobi, continued. After several false leads, Jacobi was found alive and healthy, living near Niagara, Ontario. The Louies lost no time in contacting him and arranging to fly him to Vancouver. He arrived in December 1995 and was welcomed and hosted by the entire Louie clan, eager to learn whatever they could from him.

The story, as drawn from official reports, logbooks and Jacobi's first-hand account is this: It was a night raid over Magdeburg. Bad weather broke up the formation and Quan's aircraft was soon flying alone, arriving several minutes behind the others in the group. Over Magdeburg the Halifax dropped its

CHAPTER 17

A Proud Legacy

Hok Yat Louie, cleaving to Chinese tradition, had a dream of creating a great family enterprise that would live beyond him. From humble beginnings he worked hard to build a successful business he could pass on to his oldest Canadian son, Tim, hoping it would continue to grow and be passed on to the next generation. Hok Yat never knew that the torch would land in Tong's hands, and he would build the family business into a corporation that would in 2002 rank as the fourth largest in BC—big enough to surpass the province's largest forestry company and eventually join the World Economic Forum, an exclusive organization of the world's 1,000 foremost companies.

Tong never flaunted his wealth and took every precaution to ensure that his companies would remain privately owned by the family. Imbued with the values of an older generation dedicated to an unflinching work ethic, he expressed his doubts occasionally when the subject of the new generation came up. In his later years, Tong was concerned by what he perceived to be the loss of strong traditional values, evidence of family breakdown, and failure to subscribe to a dedicated work ethic. He felt that few of the new generation

would be able to, or would want to, accept the demanding requirements that had driven him.

Ed Hellinger, who had many years in which to get to know Tong, said, "Tong was the principal force in the entire Louie clan. He set high standards and expectations for himself and for his children. It must have been hard for his offspring to grow in the shadow of a mountain. His personal example and self-discipline were difficult to equal or excel."

Many things drove Tong and one of them was his father's dream of an ongoing family enterprise. Whether he liked it or not, the time was approaching when he must finally drop the reins. It was painful to realize that he must leave the dream in other hands, no matter how promising the successor.

As if to fend off this time of reckoning, Tong continued to work with all the energy he could muster. He coped impatiently with the attrition of diabetes as well as the pain caused by his car accident injuries and an arm he broke during a hiking trip on a Caribbean island. Illness and injury were impositions he did not accept gracefully and did his best to ignore. Few knew of his diabetic condition. He maintained with a smile that he was a perpetual 39, avoiding any questions relating to his age. Even in his eighties he would grin and say, "I'm 39 . . . what does age have to do with anything?" Secretly though, aging was a concern. His father had died young; three of his brothers were dead, and Tong needed a long life to accomplish all the things he had in mind.

Robert Curry, who worked out with him at the YMCA for years, confirmed Tong's determination to be fit and to convey the impression of fitness. "Make no mistake about it, he was in great shape," Curry said. "At 75 he was going through workouts that would test a 50-year-old. Diabetes had affected his eyesight though, even if he tried to conceal the fact."

Curry remembers the time he met with Tong in London, England, during one of Tong's business junkets. "We had an evening together," he said. "My age had caught up with me and I had developed chronic knee problems. Tong was having trouble with his eyes. There we were, walking through London at dusk in a driving rainstorm. I am steering Tong by the arm, and he is acting as my crutch. I suppose you could say we were a miserable pair. Up ahead we spotted a theatre marquee advertising *Les Miserables*. We decided to see it."

Bad eyesight or not, Tong continued to work out at the YMCA up until six months before he died at the age of 84. He also continued working and being involved with numerous boards, foundations and committees. He was a Western Forest Products board member, a Saint Paul's Hospital trustee as well as chairman of the quality assurance committee for the hospital. Having served as the vice-president of development for the Vancouver Symphony Orchestra Society in 1985 and 1986, he remained one of its directors. He also remained on the board of the Sun Yat-Sen Classical Chinese Gardens, was a member of the UBC board of governors, a director of the Pacific Otolaryngology Foundation, a member of the board of governors of the Business Council of BC, a lifetime member of the Vancouver Board of Trade, to name only a few.

"It is a sign of his character that he finds the well-deserved accolades and glowing praise somewhat embarrassing," was one of the comments made in 1990, when he was given an honorary Doctor of Laws degree from the University of British Columbia. He continued to be embarrassed in the years that followed. In June 1991, he received the Order of British Columbia, a companion piece to his Order of Canada. In 1992, the Brotherhood Interfaith Society designated him Man of the Year. It was a unanimous endorsement of Tong's leadership in gaining minority recognition by combined Jewish, Catholic and Protestant service organizations.

In February 1995, Tong was the first person outside of the United States to receive IGA's prestigious J. Frank Grimes Award, named in honour of one of the parent company's founders. He was 81 at the time although he repeated his well-worn claim to be 39.

DESPITE THE DISCOMFORT OF DIABETES AND THE LOSS OF HIS BELOVED WIFE, TONG MAINTAINED HIS SENSE OF HUMOUR IN HIS LAST YEARS.

INNOVATION. No other word quite captures the spirit of London Drugs. Since its inception in 1945, London Drugs has been on the cutting edge of the retail industry, continuously searching for new ways to meet the needs of an increasingly sophisticated population. Back in the 1950s this meant introducing cameras; in the 1980s, one-hour photo finishing services and computers; in 2000, the creation of London Air Services, a charter plane company that takes people where they need to go in a hurry.

"The Vancouver-based chartered airline is cutting a swathe through the upmarket charter air business," reported the *Province* newspaper in March 2002. The airline boasts three luxury airplanes including two Learjet 45s and a 12-passenger Challenger 604. The Challenger can fly to Asia and Europe non-stop and its sumptuous interior includes leather seats, couches that convert to beds, private attendants upon request and even a putting green to help the time fly by.

So far business has been good. In addition to ferrying busy company executives, sporting stars like golfer Jesper Parnevik and movie stars like Al Pacino have turned to London Air Services to take them into the wild blue yonder.

"I have been described by some as a self-made man," he said. "One definition of a self-made man is that he is the result of unskilled labour. I tend to agree that I am missing a few nails, and there's a lot of sanding and polishing yet to be done. But until I get the job right, retirement is not an option. Don't any of you hold your breath."

The following year, as if to drive the point home a little further about not retiring, he received British Columbia's Entrepreneur of the Year award for the second time in eight years.

"Louie wants more than anything to be known as the ordinary, hard-working chairman and chief executive officer of H.Y. Louie Co. Limited and London Drugs Limited," a *BC Business* magazine article stated, "a simple man who enjoys watching pro basketball on television and playing the occasional weekend round of golf. But...his many friends consider him much more than just one of the guys. To them he is the ultimate human being, an erudite broker of goodwill who oozes tremendous warmth and unwavering loyalty."

At the award ceremony Tong again told his audience that it was unnecessary to give him awards for things he enjoyed doing: "It's a little like receiving a medal for robbing a candy store," he said. "I recommend community involvement to all of you, for the good of your health and your business." He also used the occasion to observe, "I have been able, over the years, to put something back into the community one way or another. I can recommend the practice to you. It's therapeutic. Awards are not the priority. They are just the icing on the cake. It's the community involvement that keeps me going."

In November 1996, he attended a YMCA event to witness the opening of the Bill Louie South Slope Fitness Centre, named in honour of his brother. Tong was genuinely appreciative. "I can't think of a more suitable way to remember my brother, Bill," he said. "There

were nine boys in our family. All of us were interested in sports, Bill most of all."

He had attended a ceremony earlier that year at the YWCA, where he and others were thanked for making generous donations. Tong gave a speech, and in it he tipped his hat to another one of the YWCA's donors who was seated in the audience. Wingo Wong, then 104 years old, chuckled as he listened to Tong confess that he played poker in the back of Wingo's little Chinatown drugstore 65 years earlier.

"He was a true friend," said Tong. "He never told my dad." He added that being a donor was easier than signing up for one of the Y's aerobic classes. Then he and Wong found a quiet corner to exchange memories.

Many of Tong's charities will never be revealed. His secretaries, Sheila Armstrong and Anne Stroh, spent time each working day fielding phone calls and opening mail petitioning Tong and his companies for assistance of one kind or another. Tong would review these with them on a regular basis, select the causes that seemed most deserving and start the wheels moving to investigate further. Only his public endowments are known. In addition to Saint Paul's Hospital Foundation, the Pacific Otolaryngology Foundation, the YMCA and YWCA, the Vancouver Symphony Orchestra Society, UBC and the Sun Yat-Sen Classical Chinese Gardens, Tong also supported the BC Heart Foundation, the Lions' Timmy Telethon, the Canadian Diabetic Association, Crime Stoppers of Greater Vancouver, the Salvation Army and the Tong Louie Heart Unit at Saint Paul's Hospital. In 1995, he presented a gift to the Library Square Capital Campaign enabling the installation of the Tong Louie Reading Gallery in the new Vancouver Library.

In his final years he made major grants to institutions directly concerned with health and longevity. The first of these, established in April 1993, was the Geraldine and Tong Louie Human Performance Centre at Simon Fraser University's Harbour Centre

in downtown Vancouver. The centre conducts a variety of programs including teaching, research and community service dealing with health, fitness, occupational health and safety; all aspects of this directed to seniors' needs to a substantial degree.

Finally, on Friday, November 7, 1997, he took part in the opening of the Dr. Tong Louie Living Laboratory, a $1.1-million joint research project of the Simon Fraser University's Gerontology Research Centre and the British Columbia Institute of Technology's Technology Centre. The laboratory focuses on the development of devices, housing designs and furnishings intended to enable elderly and disabled persons to live independently.

In making the gift, Tong explained, "when I considered the fact that, in 20 years or so I might be a candidate for some of the things generated by the Living Laboratory, I suddenly decided it was an extremely worthwhile cause, and I was more than happy to contribute to it."

By the time he said this, it was becoming increasingly apparent to his family, friends and colleagues that his physical ailments were overtaking him. Diabetes was working its inexorable damage, causing his already bad eyesight to worsen. His energy level was waning, even though he continued with his regular workouts and kept up his business routine. As far as Tong was concerned, it was business as usual and his physical condition was not a matter for discussion. Then, in early 1998, his health declined markedly. Problems relating to his diabetes forced him to enter the hospital for tests and observation and he was given medication that did little to help him. In fact, the side effects were so debilitating he had to give up his workouts and cut back on business routines already made difficult by his fading vision.

On January 12, 1998, he was admitted to hospital once more. The prognosis was not good. He remained in the hospital for several weeks until it was decided that he would be more comfortable in his own surroundings. There was nothing the hospital could do that could not be achieved by good nursing care in his own home. He returned to his home on February 28, 1998.

His secretary visited him each day, enabling him to carry on a semblance of business. Friends and family members stopped by, careful to limit their visits in view of his failing energy and attention span. His birthday on March 1 was a low-key affair, its significance lost in the struggle he was enduring—a struggle he was losing. April saw him totally weakened, comatose much of the time, and barely able to respond to visits when he was conscious. On April 28, 1998, he passed away.

The young man who had taken his father's dream out of a Chinatown ghetto and guided it into one of the country's most successful corporations had finally laid down the reins, but he left his father's dream of a great family enterprise in capable hands.

In an interview Brandt Louie revealed clearly that he understood and accepted the challenge. "There's been a common vision right from my grandfather's day," he said. "We're trying to build something that will last for generations into the future. That's an integral element of Chinese culture.

"Each generation has a responsibility to ensure that the next generation will be more successful. Just like my grandfather and my father, my dream is to create a legacy to pass on to my children. I have inherited my father's good name and business. It's not mine to squander. I have to build something to pass on. That's an inbred duty."

During Tong's last days tributes poured in from all quarters but voiced a common theme: BC had lost a titan it hardly knew. *The Vancouver Sun* ran a full-page story headed: "Vancouver mourns a man who refused to acknowledge barriers: Louie's life of charity changed a city." David Lam, the former lieutenant-governor and

fellow philanthropist, said Tong's generation had paved the way for the success of men like himself because "they have gone through hardship and held their place." Roy Mah, legendary publisher of the *Chinatown News* said Tong was one of the first individuals who was determined to integrate into greater Vancouver society, largely by refusing to acknowledge the barriers before him.

"In the early days, when it wasn't so easy to assimilate, he sort of blazed the trail for future generations to follow," said Mah.

Lam added that Tong was a model of business success and public generosity. "When Tong Louie acquired London Drugs I felt personally some sort of pride," he said. "And when he was appointed to the board of the Royal Bank, the Chinese community that I knew, we actually celebrated." Here was a man born in the days when his people were, in Liang Ch'i-ch'ao's words, "treated like cattle, horses and slaves" living to be invited into the nation's most exclusive circles of power.

"My goodness," said Lam. "This was like crossing a bridge."

It was a bridge Tong had spent his life building, and it wasn't just a bridge to wealth and influence.

Perhaps the most impressive tributes of all were the thousands who turned out in person to say goodbye to this man who had touched them in their own lives, and the thousands more around the province and around the world who made their own very personal farewells. For Tong had never forgotten his father's teaching that people are the greatest wealth, and he had never stopped building bridges between them and between their cultures.

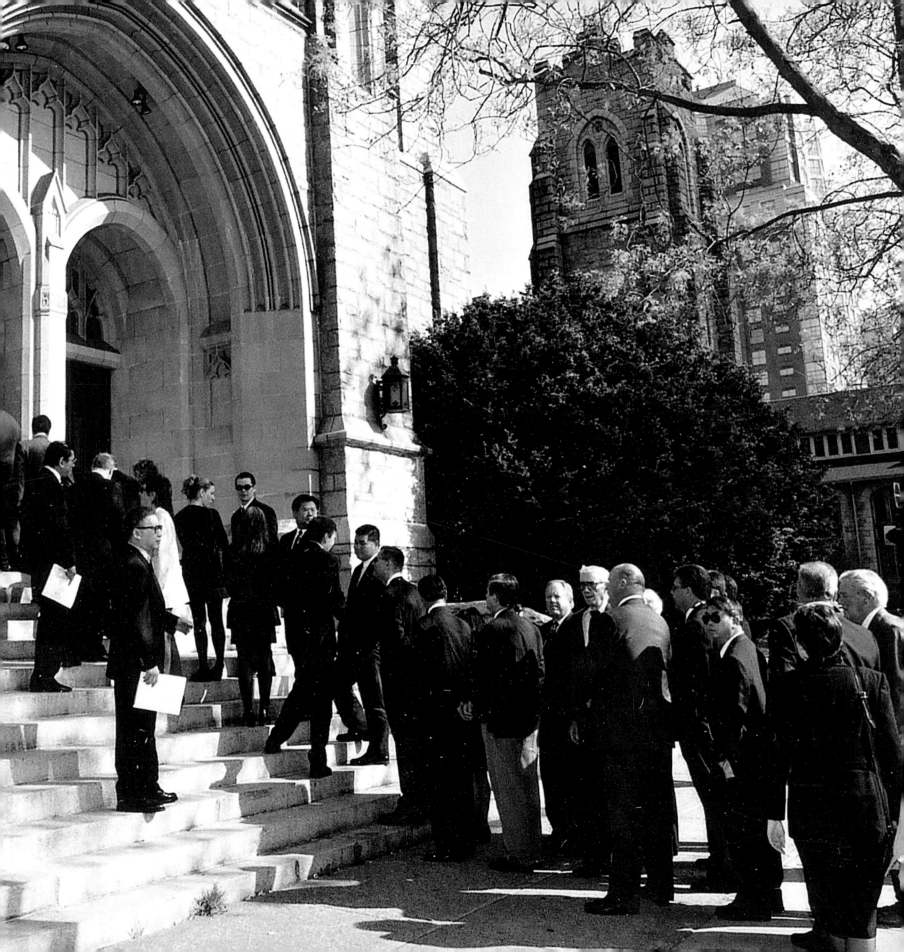

Index

Published by
Harbour Publishing Co. Ltd., P.O. Box 219, Madeira Park, BC V0N 2H0
www.harbourpublishing.com

Edited by Nadine Pedersen and Howard White
Cover and page design and layout by Martin Nichols

Photo credits:
All photographs are part of the H.Y. Louie Co. Limited, London Drugs or Louie family collections unless otherwise specified. All photographs belonging to the City of Vancouver Archives=CVA, Canadian Grocer Archives=CGA, the Vancouver Public Library, Special Collections=VPL. Front cover Kirk McGregor for the Nucomm Group, back cover Ron Sangha, author photograph Michelle Perrault, 6-7 Pat Higinbotham, 9 (Vancouver Sun), 18 (Harbour Publishing), 19 (VPL 12866), 20 (VPL 1746), 21 (VPL 19977), 22 (VPL 1773), 25 (VPL 210), 26 (VPL 17063), 28 (VPL 7742), 29 (VPL 19867), 30 (CVA 352-7), 31 (CVA 677-27), 32 (CVA Dist. N157), 33 (James Crookall, CVA 260-735), 35 (VPL 6729), 36 (James Crookall, CVA 260-737), 38 (CVA 260-242), 39 top (CVA Van Sc N. 66#1 VLP 8), 39 bottom (VPL 939), 42 (VPL 2008), 49 (CVA 371-809), 50 (VPL 12720), 52 (VPL 20389), 57 (Stuart Thomson, CVA 99-2466), 58 (CVA Port N. 1218 P. 1758), 60 (VPL 12749), 61 (VPL 8813), 62 (James Crookall, CVA 260-316), 63 (VPL 11792), 68 (James Crookall, CVA 260-2), 75 (CVA Bu N206), 76 (Paul Trussell collection), 82 (VPL 4693), 95 (CVA 300-25), 101 (CVA 1184-3045), 102 (CVA 354-123), 116 CGA, 123 CGA, 127 (VPL 2002), 163 CGA, 185 (Gail Buente, courtesy of the Dr. Sun Yat-Sen Classical Chinese Garden).

Acknowledgements:
This book would have been impossible without the full and enthusiastic co-operation of family, relatives, friends and business associates who contributed their recollections of a valued friend and colleague.

Thanks must go as well to staff members of the Vancouver Public Library, the Library of the University of British Columbia and the British Columbia Provincial Archives. Thanks also to Howard White and Nadine Pedersen. Special mention must be directed to Debbie Tardiff and Anne Stroh whose tireless and efficient efforts as intermediaries and collaborators were greatly appreciated.

The editors would like to add their thanks to Nathen Shandler in the London Drugs audio visual department who went the extra distance to help illustrate the book, Tim Louie for the opportunity to read his unpublished paper on Hok Yat Louie, to Willis Louie for his cheerful and patient assistance, to Jim Wong Chu for his invaluable perspective on Chinese-Canadian history, to Wynne Powell of London Drugs, whose efficient facilitation was instrumental, and finally to Brandt Louie without whose perseverance and support this book would not have come to be.

Printed in Canada

Harbour Publishing acknowledges the financial support of the Government of Canada through the Book Publishing Industry Development Program (BPIDP) and the Canada Council for the Arts, and the Province of British Columbia through the British Columbia Arts Council, for its publishing activities.

The Canada Council | Le Conseil des Arts
for the Arts | du Canada
since 1957 | depuis 1957

National Library of Canada Cataloguing in Publication Data

Perrault, E. G. (Ernest G.)
  Tong : the story of Tong Louie, Vancouver's quiet titan / Ernest Perrault.

Includes index.
ISBN 1-55017-231-X

1. Louie, Tong, 1914-1998. 2. Businessmen-British Columbia — Vancouver — Biography.
3. Chinese Canadians-British Columbia — Vancouver — Biography. 4. Vancouver (B.C.) — Biography. I. Title.
FC3847.26.L68P47   2002 971.1'3304'092   C2002-911302-4   F1089.5.V22P47 2002

便如公暇時裁章答之以慰之念並讀鋪

中佳意近況若何詳細論及此候

文濤道兄　鄉弟五古頓中